WHERE THE ACTION IS

An Easy ESL Approach to Pure Regular Verbs

by
Lawrence Klepinger, M.A. Ed.

BARRON'S

OCT 30 2001

DOUGLAS COLLEGE LIBRARIES

© Copyright 1997, 1998 by Lawrence Klepinger

All rights reserved.

No part of this book may be reproduced in any form, by photostat, microfilm, xerography, or any other means, or incorporated into any information retrieval system, electronic or mechanical, without the written permission of the copyright owner.

All inquiries should be addressed to:
Barron's Educational Series, Inc.
250 Wireless Boulevard
Hauppauge, New York 11788
http://www.barronseduc.com

Library of Congress Catalog Card No.: 98-5899

International Standard Book No. 0-7641-0509-4

Library of Congress Cataloging-in-Publication Data

Klepinger, Lawrence.
    Where the action is (pure regular verbs) / by Lawrence Klepinger.
        p. cm.
    ISBN 0-7641-0509-4
    1. English language—Verb—Problems, exercises, etc.   I. Title.
PE1271.K57 1998
428.2—dc21   98-5899
                                                                CIP

PRINTED IN THE UNITED STATES OF AMERICA

9 8 7 6 5 4 3 2 1

Table of Contents

To the Student

This textbook is designed to be student/teacher friendly.

The purpose of this book is to help you learn, in an easy way, how to use pure American English verbs and conjugate them correctly in everyday written and spoken communication.

You are learning not only verbs but also other words, phrases, and useful expressions. Through careful study you will increase your overall English ability in a relatively short period of time.

Please make sure to read the section "How This Book Is Organized" and the "Introduction."

With a little practice, it's easy.

Good luck—and don't give up!

To the Teacher

Brief Description of the Highlights of This Textbook:

1. You can photocopy any part of this book for classroom use.
2. No teacher's text is needed.
3. The format is self-explanatory and easy-to-use.
4. This is not a grammar book.
5. The conjugated verbs in this text were chosen because they are multifunctional.
6. A Student Worksheet is included for easy, out-of-book studying and grading.
7. Tests are already prepared, with Answer Keys included.

Detailed Description of the Highlights of This Textbook:

1. *Where The Action Is* is designed to be very student/teacher friendly; you have permission to copy any portion of it for use in class.
2. This book is self-explanatory, so no teacher's text is needed, thus affording total freedom and flexibility to the instructor.
3. It is designed for immediate and practical use by both student and teacher alike.
4. This is not a grammar book; therefore, no distinctions are made between gerunds, infinitives, auxiliaries, modals, transitive or intransitive verbs, active or passive voice nor are any other strict grammatical points emphasized. Emphasis is placed only on practical usage of verbs: their proper tense, correct spelling, their use as nouns (where appropriate) and their use in phrases and expressions.
5. The verbs that are conjugated in this series were chosen because they are multifunctional. That is, they can be used as a verb or a noun, or have useful expressions associated with them. The teacher is encouraged to use as many verbs in this text as possible, not just the ones that have already been fully conjugated. This gives the teacher complete freedom to work with students to add to the verbs that are already conjugated in this book.

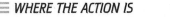

6 There is a **Student Worksheet** on page 5 that can be photocopied, used in class, and then collected to monitor how well the students are doing. Not only is this a great way to help structure each student's approach to mastering verbs, it also makes sure that everybody is "on the same page" at the same time. Furthermore, the worksheet is also very handy as an extra handout and affords the teacher the freedom and flexibility to use the blackboard in class to expand on verb usage, how the verb is used as a noun, and also to discuss other useful expressions using the target verb. Finally, using this worksheet allows students to construct their own verb workbook right in class.

7 The **Midterm Test** and all five **Comprehensive Tests** have been prepared with answer keys included. As with all other material in this text, you can photocopy them and use them as tests in the classroom. The **Answer Key** starts on page 119.

Note

For maximum results, I tell my students to study either the Midterm Test or all five Comprehensive Tests before the appropriate examination period. This way they are guaranteed to put in directed, quality study time, learn the specified pages, and feel confident in taking the examination on what they have studied. Some teachers have had good results creating customized tests by selecting their "favorite" sections from various exams. Feel free to experiment.

You can't get much more student/teacher friendly than *Where the Action Is*. Virtually all the work is done for you. All you have to do is pick a verb and go for it. You have total freedom to handle its presentation any way you wish.

Please make sure to read the section "How This Book Is Organized" and also the "Introduction." You might even want to cover them in class with your students. I have found this approach to work very well.

Acknowledgments

I would like to thank the following people for helping me to make this book possible.

Bill and Beth Mansell, ESL Instructors, for taking a tremendous amount of time out of their teaching schedules to help me with my many computer problems, and also for agreeing to pilot test this textbook.

Scott Greene, ESL Instructor, for his insight and patience in reading over the entire manuscript and pointing out problem areas while helping me to correct them, and also for agreeing to pilot test this textbook in all of his ESL English classes.

Brian and Aminta Peters, ESL Instructors, for their help, computer expertise, and encouragement on the writing of this book, and also for their insight and critical comments that helped bring this project together.

Lawrence E. and Charles I. Kelly, ESL Instructors, at the Internet TESL Journal, **http://www.aitech.ac.jp/~iteslj/**, for their support and Internet acumen. And also, thanks for their positive review of this text on their Internet home page.

Michael Kruse, RSA Dip., for his help and inspiration and also for agreeing to pilot test the text in his ESL classes.

Susan Gilfert, former Fulbright Lecturer and author of *TOEIC Strategies*, for her insightful comments and willingness to pilot test the text in her ESL classes.

Alice Parker, Director of Communications, International Learning Systems, Inc., for constantly giving me her professional ideas and comments free of charge.

All my ESL students who offered many constructive suggestions after allowing me to use this text as a pilot project in my classes.

As always, my wife, Akiko, and daughter, Mai, for their endless support and encouragement.

And a special thanks to my editor at Barron's Educational Series, Inc., Linda Turner, for her straightforward approach, honest suggestions, candid criticism, and most of all, great sense of humor.

How This Book Is Organized

1 *Where The Action Is* shows the different spelling of verbs with an easy-to-understand verb conjugation chart, thus eliminating spelling mistakes.

Example:

verb	"s" form	Present Participle	Past	Past Participle
act	acts	acting	acted	acted

2 Sample sentences show the easy conjugation of the verb.

3 In many cases this book also shows how the verb is used as a(n);
  a. noun,
  b. affirmative or negative statement,
  c. question,
  d. part of useful words and expressions. These useful words and expressions can be used either as slang, colloquialisms, or idiomatic expressions. Also, sometimes there will be easy-to-remember phrasal verbs that are used in context. *To keep it simple, they are all collectively referred to as "Useful Words and Expressions."*

4 Definitions of the verbs are kept simple, as are the other uses of the verbs.

5 Finally, the student is given the chance to write his or her own sentence for each of the conjugated forms of the verb.

Full-Page Example:

bank • to deposit money; to do business with a financial institution

bank	banks	banking	banked	banked

Verb

① We **bank** our money here every Friday.

② That company **banks** with a very small savings and loan.

③ She does all her **banking** overseas.

④ He **banked** there for 20 years.

⑤ Hasn't the secretary already **banked** the money?

Noun

bank • a financial institution where money is borrowed, withdrawn, or deposited; the area of land alongside a river

　① Our **bank** is open on Saturday.

　② While my sister was fishing, she walked along the **bank**.

Useful Words and Expressions

bank(ing) on • to depend on something or someone to do something
　*I'm **banking on** her to turn the company around.*

Now write your own sentences

① **bank**　　•　_____

② **banks**　•　_____

③ **banking** •　_____

④ **banked** • _____

⑤ **banked** • _____

6 From time to time there is also a **NOTE:** within the text to make a specific point when needed.

7 In recent years American English has become the most widely accepted form of English usage. Therefore, all verbs, and their subsequent conjugations, are presented in the American English format.

8 There are two easy-to-understand charts on pages 3 and 4 to help the student with proper conjugation.

9 Each verb can be found in the **Master Verb List** at the very back of this book, starting on page 123. All verbs are listed alphabetically. Verbs that are fully conjugated and used as examples throughout this book appear in bold type.

Introduction

Pure Regular Verbs

This textbook only concerns itself with Pure Regular Verbs.

> A **Pure Regular Verb** is any verb that needs *only* the addition of **s**, **ing**, **ed**, or **ed** to fully conjugate the verb.

If any verb does not follow this definition, it is not considered a Pure Regular Verb and will not be covered in this textbook.

Example:

verb	+ s	+ ing	+ ed	+ ed
call	calls	calling	called	called

Verbs Show Action or State of Being

Example: Action

> He **called** for help.

This example shows Action, that is, *called*.

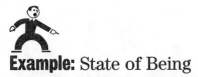
Example: State of Being

> This **is** my home.

This example shows a State of (something or someone) Being, that is, *is*.

Verb Tense

Verb tense shows when an Action or State of Being takes place.

Example:

---

① The student **studied**. (Simple Past/Action)

② She **is** home. (Simple Present/State of Being)

Full Verb Conjugation

Present Tense			
Present Simple	**Present Progressive**	**Present Perfect**	**Present Perfect Progressive**
(+) You talk.	You are talking.	You have talked.	You have been talking.
(-) You do not talk.	You are not talking.	You have not talked.	You have not been talking.
(?) Do you talk?	Are you talking?	Have you talked?	Have you been talking?
Past Tense			
Past Simple	**Past Progressive**	**Past Perfect**	**Past Perfect Progressive**
(+) She talked.	She was talking.	She had talked.	She had been talking.
(-) She did not talk.	She was not talking.	She had not talked.	She had not been talking.
(?) Did she talk?	Was she talking?	Had she talked?	Had she been talking?
Future Tense			
Future Simple	**Future Progressive**	**Future Perfect**	**Future Perfect Progressive**
(+) I will talk.	I will be talking.	I will have talked.	I will have been talking.
(-) I will not talk.	I will not be talking.	I will not have talked.	I will not have been talking.
(?) Will I talk?	Will I be talking?	Will I have talked?	Will I have been talking?

day	the day before yesterday	yesterday	today	tomorrow	the day after tomorrow	every day
morning	the morning before last	yesterday morning	this morning	tomorrow morning	the morning after next	every morning
afternoon	the afternoon before last	yesterday afternoon	this afternoon	tomorrow afternoon	the afternoon after next	every afternoon
evening	the evening before last	yesterday evening	this evening	tomorrow evening	the evening after next	every evening
night	the night before last	last night	tonight	tomorrow night	the night after next	every night
week	the week before last	last week	this week	next week	the week after next	every week
month	the month before last	last month	this month	next month	the month after next	every month
year	the year before last	last year	this year	next year	the year after next	every year

Student Worksheet #___

Student Name _____

Student Number _____

Verb/Definition

_____ • _____

Now write your own sentences

① _____ • _____

② _____ • _____

③ _____ • _____

④ _____ • _____

⑤ _____ • _____

Noun

_____ • _____

_____ • _____

Useful Words and Expressions

① _____

② _____

③ _____

Pure Regular Verbs

act • to perform in a play or movie production; to respond in a certain way; to pretend in some form or manner; to perform some job or function

act	acts	acting	acted	acted

Verb

① They **act** in the play.

② He **acts** like he doesn't know her.

③ She is **acting** as his attorney.

④ The man **acted** very strangely.

⑤ Her daughter had never **acted** in a movie before.

Noun

act • one part of a play, performance, or stage production

The play had only one **act**.

Useful Words and Expressions

acting up • not working right

*My computer is **acting up** again.*

get your act together • to get organized

*If you want to keep your job, you'd better **get your act together**.*

Now write your own sentences

① act • _____

② acts • _____

③ acting • _____

④ acted • _____

⑤ acted • _____

answer • to reply to a question

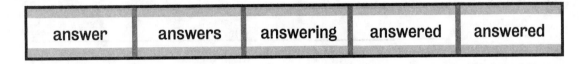

answer	answers	answering	answered	answered

Verb

① Can you **answer** the question?

② That student never **answers** in class.

③ He was **answering** the telephone.

④ My mother **answered** my father's letter yesterday.

⑤ Have you already **answered**?

Noun

answer • the reply to a question

Do you know what the **answer** is?

Useful Words and Expressions

answering machine • an automatic machine that takes telephone messages

*My **answering machine** isn't working.*

answering service • a service company that screens all incoming calls and takes messages

*Their **answering service** is very good.*

to know all the answers • when a person thinks he or she knows everything

*My professor thinks he **knows all the answers**.*

Now write your own sentences

① **answer** • _____

② **answers** • _____

③ **answering** • _____

④ **answered** • _____

⑤ **answered** • _____

ask • to state a question

ask	asks	asking	asked	asked

Verb

① Would you like to **ask** a question?

② He **asks** every girl for a date.

③ The mayor was **asking** people to vote for him.

④ I **asked** them for directions.

⑤ Our doctor has never **asked** for money.

Useful Words and Expressions

asking for it • trying to start trouble; initiating a possibly dangerous situation or outcome

① *That new kid keeps **asking for it**.*

② *You're **asking for it** if you call in sick.*

asking price • the retail price of something; starting price

*The **asking price** is too expensive.*

Now write your own sentences

① **ask** • _____

② **asks** • _____

③ **asking** • _____

④ **asked** • _____

⑤ **asked** • _____

attack • to challenge by going forward; to display extremely aggressive behavior; to try to injure or kill something or someone

attack	attacks	attacking	attacked	attacked

Verb

① The soldiers will **attack** tomorrow evening.
② My neighbor's dog always **attacks** the mail carrier.
③ He was **attacking** her verbally by screaming insults.
④ Did you say the wolf **attacked** the chickens?
⑤ The army hasn't **attacked**.

Noun

attack • assault or military assault; a seizure by disease or illness

① They planned the **attack** in secret.
② My grandfather had a heart **attack**.

Now write your own sentences

① **attack** • _____

② **attacks** • _____

③ **attacking** • _____

④ **attacked** • _____

⑤ **attacked** • _____

back • to go in a reverse direction; to return; to support someone or something

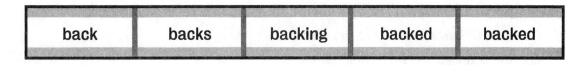

| back | backs | backing | backed | backed |

Verb

① I'm going to **back** the car into the garage.
② She **backs** the new idea.
③ The boxer kept **backing** away.
④ His friends **backed** up what he said.
⑤ Had the boy **backed** away he would have been safe.

Noun

back • the rear part of the body from the shoulders to the hips; a place or position not in front

① My **back** hurts.
② The celebrity sat in the **back** of the theater.

Useful Words and Expressions

back door • a door located at the back of a house or building
*The thief sneaked in the **back door**.*

back down • to admit defeat; to withdraw from a fight
*The senator would never **back down** from an argument.*

back off • to quit doing or saying something; to quit being aggressive
*I wish he would **back off** a little.*

back seat • the seat behind the front seat in a vehicle
*Put your child in the **back seat**.*

back-seat driver • a person who is always telling someone else how to drive a car while riding as a passenger

*My mother is a terrible **back-seat driver**.*

back up • to give support or agree with; to move in a reverse direction

① *He will **back up** my statement.*

② *She **backed up** the truck.*

Now write your own sentences

① **back** • _____

② **backs** • _____

③ **backing** • _____

④ **backed** • _____

⑤ **backed** • _____

bank • to deposit money; to do business with a financial institution

bank	banks	banking	banked	banked

Verb

① We **bank** our money here every Friday.
② That company **banks** with a very small savings and loan.
③ She does all her **banking** overseas.
④ He **banked** there for 20 years.
⑤ Hasn't the secretary already **banked** the money?

Noun

bank • a financial institution where money is borrowed, withdrawn, or deposited; the area of land along the side of a river
  ① Our **bank** is open on Saturday.
  ② While my sister was fishing, she walked along the **bank**.

Useful Words and Expressions

bank(ing) on • to depend on something or someone to do something
  *We are **banking on** her to turn the company around.*
take that to the bank • something that is guaranteed; for sure; no doubt
  *I'm going to work hard, and you can **take that to the bank**.*

Now write your own sentences

① **bank** • _____

② **banks** • _____

③ **banking** • _____

④ **banked** • _____

⑤ **banked** • _____

bark • to make the sharp cry that a dog makes; to speak sharply

bark	barks	barking	barked	barked

Verb

① Does your dog **bark** at night?
② My father **barks** at everybody.
③ We got angry because our neighbor's dog was always **barking**.
④ The drill sergeant **barked** out his orders.
⑤ Her new puppy hasn't **barked** once.

Noun

bark • the tough protective outer layer of trees and shrubs

The tree's **bark** was used for medicine.

Useful Words and Expressions

one's bark is worse than one's bite • not as dangerous as one seems

*Don't worry, the director's **bark is worse than her bite**.*

bark(ing) up the wrong tree • to make an effort in the wrong direction; to be mistakenly on the wrong track

*You are **barking up the wrong tree** if you think I am guilty.*

Now write your own sentences

① **bark** • _____

② **barks** • _____

③ **barking** • _____

④ **barked** • _____

⑤ **barked** • _____

block • to stop someone or something from doing something

block	blocks	blocking	blocked	blocked

Verb

① The politician tried to **block** every move his opponent made.

② The football team's defensive line **blocks** very well.

③ A traffic accident is **blocking** the highway.

④ Guards **blocked** the exit.

⑤ No one has **blocked** her promotion.

Noun

block • a solid piece of material, usually of stone or rock; an area in a city or town

① The house was made of cement **blocks**.

② We both live on the same **block**.

Useful Words and Expressions

blockbuster • a great movie or book

*Every movie she produces is a **blockbuster**.*

blockhead • a stupid person

*Sometimes my friend is a real **blockhead**.*

block letters • all capital letters; upper-case letters

*Please write your full name in **BLOCK LETTERS**.*

mental block • unable to remember something

*My boss seemed to have a **mental block** when I asked him about my pay raise.*

writer's block • inability of a writer to think of anything to write

*The author had a bad case of **writer's block**.*

Now write your own sentences

① **block**   • _____

② **blocks**   • _____

③ **blocking**   • _____

④ **blocked**   • _____

⑤ **blocked**   • _____

borrow • to take something with the intent of giving it back; to receive something with the intent of paying it back; to get a loan

borrow	borrows	borrowing	borrowed	borrowed

Verb

① My brother wants to **borrow** some money from me.
② Her boyfriend **borrows** her car every day.
③ It is not easy **borrowing** money from a bank.
④ I **borrowed** the book yesterday evening.
⑤ Haven't you ever **borrowed** money before?

Useful Words and Expressions

borrowing power • the ability to borrow money with good credit
   *His new company doesn't have much **borrowing power**.*

borrowed time • to be running out of time; to be in serious trouble
   *The government is living on **borrowed time**.*

Now write your own sentences

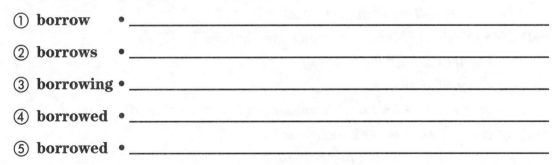

① **borrow**   • _____

② **borrows**   • _____

③ **borrowing** • _____

④ **borrowed** • _____

⑤ **borrowed** • _____

call • to cry out loud; to get attention with a loud voice; to phone someone

call	calls	calling	called	called

Verb

① Please don't **call** my name in public.

② My father always **calls** me when I am asleep.

③ Mr. Johnson is **calling** from Alaska.

④ The child **called** out to his mother.

⑤ She hasn't **called** yet.

Noun

call • a telephone call

There is a **call** for Dr. Smith on line one.

Useful Words and Expressions

call back • to return a telephone call later

She'll **call back** this evening.

call collect • a telephone call paid for by the person receiving the call

I never **call collect** to my parents.

call off • to cancel or stop something from happening

You'd better **call off** the meeting.

call on • to visit someone

He's going to **call on** his sick aunt in the hospital this afternoon.

calling card • business card; name card

The new salesperson left her **calling card**.

on call • not actually working but ready to work if needed

The doctor is **on call** tonight.

Now write your own sentences

① **call** • _____

② **calls** • _____

③ **calling** • _____

④ **called** • _____

⑤ **called** • _____

check • to investigate or look into something; to inquire; to make a mark in writing

check	checks	checking	checked	checked

Verb

① **Check** to see if the gas is off.
② His daughter **checks** the mail every day.
③ The tour guide is **checking** off the names.
④ All the items on the list were **checked** by the clerk.
⑤ The detective has already **checked** that room.

Noun

check • a mark or sign; a financial instrument used in place of money; a bill in a restaurant

① The traveler made a **check** next to his name on the list.
② She wrote a **check** for $1,000.
③ He asked the waiter for the **check**.

Useful Words and Expressions

checkbook • a book that holds unused bank checks

*I lost my **checkbook**.*

checking account • a money account at a bank

*I hope I have enough money in my **checking account**.*

check in • to register for a hotel room; to register at an airport, bus, train, or ship counter

① *What time can I **check in** at the hotel?*
② *Please **check in** two hours before your flight leaves.*

check it out • to investigate thoroughly

*His story sounded strange so the boss decided to **check it out**.*

check on • to investigate thoroughly; to see how something or someone is doing or feeling

   ① *The firefighter decided to **check on** the report immediately.*

   ② *I'm going to **check on** my sister tomorrow.*

check out • to formally leave a hotel

   *Don't forget to leave the keys when you **check out**.*

checkup • a physical examination

   *I had my annual **checkup** last week.*

Now write your own sentences

  ① **check**   • _____

  ② **checks**   • _____

  ③ **checking**   • _____

  ④ **checked**   • _____

  ⑤ **checked**   • _____

cook • to prepare food by fire or heat

| cook | cooks | cooking | cooked | cooked |

Verb

① I love to **cook**.

② He **cooks** breakfast every weekend.

③ She's **cooking** dinner now.

④ Every year his grandmother **cooked** a Thanksgiving turkey.

⑤ He's never **cooked** a meal for himself?

Noun

cook • a person who prepares food to be eaten

That restaurant has the best **cook** in town.

Useful Words and Expressions

cooked up • to make false statements; to lie

*It sounds like he **cooked up** that story to protect himself.*

what's cooking? • what is happening?; what's going on?; what is taking place?

***What's cooking** for this evening?*

Now write your own sentences

① **cook** • _____

② **cooks** • _____

③ **cooking** • _____

④ **cooked** • _____

⑤ **cooked** • _____

count • to use numbers; to determine the total number

| count | counts | counting | counted | counted |

Verb

① Her young niece can **count** to 10.

② His friend **counts** every penny he makes.

③ The waiter was **counting** the guests at the party.

④ I **counted** 250 cows on the ranch.

⑤ Have you **counted** all the books in the library?

Noun

count • a foreign noble, the same as an earl

He used to brag about his grandfather being a **count** in Europe.

Useful Words and Expressions

count on • to depend on; to have faith in

*You can **count on** her to do a good job.*

count your blessings • to be happy with what you have; to be grateful

*You should **count your blessings** for being healthy.*

count your chickens • to be overly optimistic about something

*Don't **count your chickens** until you get the money.*

Now write your own sentences

① **count** • _____

② **counts** • _____

③ **counting** • _____

④ **counted** • _____

⑤ **counted** • _____

cover • to place something on or over something to protect it; to follow a story or news item

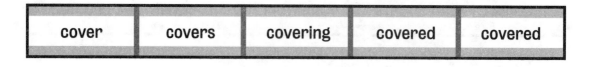

| cover | covers | covering | covered | covered |

Verb

① Make sure you **cover** the bird cage at night.
② She **covers** all the business news at 6:00 PM.
③ The farmer is **covering** the seeds with a little dirt.
④ After riding, she **covered** the horse with a wool blanket.
⑤ They've already **covered** that story.

Noun

cover • something used to protect or preserve something; used to keep warm

① The **cover** for the car was made of plastic.
② The girl's only **cover** was a light blanket.

Useful Words and Expressions

book cover • the front cover of a book; book jacket
  *The **book cover** design was very creative.*

cover-up • a plan for hiding the truth from public view
  *Is there a **cover-up** with regard to the president?*

cover yourself • to protect yourself; to be safe from harm
  *Make sure you **cover yourself** when doing your taxes.*

Now write your own sentences

1. **cover** • _____

2. **covers** • _____

3. **covering** • _____

4. **covered** • _____

5. **covered** • _____

diet • to eat a special type or amount of food and nothing else

| diet | diets | dieting | dieted | dieted |

Verb

① If you **diet** on a regular basis you will be in better health.

② My sister always **diets** after eating too much dessert.

③ **Dieting** is very difficult for me.

④ My father **dieted** all summer long and lost a lot of weight.

⑤ If he had **dieted,** he would have lived longer.

Noun

diet • the kind of food that a person habitually eats; a legislative body

① A **diet** of hamburgers and French fries is not good for you.

② Japan has a **diet** but America has a congress.

Useful Words and Expressions

to go on a diet • to eat and drink only certain things so as to lose weight
*My New Year's Resolution was **to go on a diet** and lose 20 pounds.*

to go off a diet • to break the rules of a diet and eat and drink anything
*Make sure you don't **go off your diet**.*

Now write your own sentences

① **diet** • _____

② **diets** • _____

③ **dieting** • _____

④ **dieted** • _____

⑤ **dieted** • _____

duck • to quickly get down so as not to be hit; to lower your head so as not to hit something; to go down or go under something

duck	ducks	ducking	ducked	ducked

Verb

① The boxer didn't **duck** and was knocked out.
② My brother **ducks** every time he walks through a doorway.
③ The children kept **ducking** underwater.
④ She **ducked** to miss the low hanging branch.
⑤ If he hadn't **ducked**, he would have hit his head.

Noun

duck • any kind of swimming bird with webbed feet
   Donald is the most famous **duck** in the world.

Useful Words and Expressions

duck a question • to not answer a question; to avoid a direct response
   *The vice-president is very skillful at **ducking questions**.*
duck out • to leave quickly or hide from something or someone
   *I **ducked out** of the office just before the meeting.*

Now write your own sentences

① **duck**   • _____
② **ducks**   • _____
③ **ducking**   • _____
④ **ducked**   • _____
⑤ **ducked**   • _____

hand • to deliver or give by hand

hand	hands	handing	handed	handed

Verb

① Would you please **hand** me that book?

② He **hands** all his money to his wife every payday.

③ The teacher is **handing** out the test to the class.

④ The rebels **handed** in their weapons.

⑤ He has **handed** everything to his attorney.

Noun

hand • the end part of the arm beyond the wrist, including the fingers and thumb; playing cards that are dealt to a player

① Professional basketball players have very big **hands**.

② I didn't get one good poker **hand** all night.

Useful Words and Expressions

by hand, handmade • made by a person and not a machine

① *All these ceramics were made by hand.*

② *Everything in this store is handmade.*

firsthand information • reliable information; not hearsay

The judge would accept only firsthand information.

NOTE: The opposite of firsthand information is *secondhand information*.

from hand to mouth • barely making a living; very poor

Many people in the world live from hand to mouth.

give a hand • to applaud; to clap your hands

*Let's all **give a hand** to our next speaker.*

handpick • to choose very carefully; a personal choice

*The captain **handpicked** her own staff.*

hands-on • involved in actually doing the work

*She is a real **hands-on** governor.*

to lend a hand • to help; to give assistance

*I offered **to lend a hand** with the cleaning.*

Now write your own sentences

① **hand**

② **hands**

③ **handing**

④ **handed**

⑤ **handed**

head • to be going in a certain direction; to be going toward something or someone; to lead or be in charge of

| head | heads | heading | headed | headed |

Verb

① He decided to **head** out to Colorado.
② Mrs. Anderson **heads** the accounting department.
③ Their marriage is **heading** toward disaster.
④ All the guests **headed** for the exit.
⑤ She had previously **headed** the company.

Noun

head • upper part of the body containing eyes, mouth, ears, nose and brain
   His **head** is too big for the hat.

Useful Words and Expressions

head and shoulders • by a very large amount
   *Her company is **head and shoulders** above her rivals.*

head back • to return; to turn around and go back to where one came from
   *We should **head back** before it gets dark.*

head cold • a common cold
   *This **head cold** has given me a runny nose and a sore throat.*

head-on • to challenge up front; with the front taking the force
   ① *He decided to confront the situation **head-on**.*
   ② *The two cars hit **head-on**.*

over your head • to be in trouble or in a dangerous situation
   *You'll be getting in **over your head** if you borrow too much money.*

Now write your own sentences

① **head** • _____

② **heads** • _____

③ **heading** • _____

④ **headed** • _____

⑤ **headed** • _____

help • to provide assistance; to give support

help	helps	helping	helped	helped

Verb

① My mother tries to **help** everybody.

② Her husband never **helps** around the house.

③ Everyone is **helping** to rebuild the town.

④ The young child **helped** her grandfather up the stairs.

⑤ Why haven't you ever **helped** your parents before?

Noun

help • assistance, such as from the police, fire department, or ambulance service

I called the hospital and **help** is on the way.

Useful Words and Expressions

helping hand • to lend support in a difficult situation

*The government finally decided to lend a **helping hand** to the earthquake victims.*

help yourself • to take as much as you like

*Please **help yourself** to more chocolate cake.*

Now write your own sentences

① **help** • _____

② **helps** • _____

③ **helping** • _____

④ **helped** • _____

⑤ **helped** • _____

iron • to smooth clothing with a hot object to make it look neat and clean

iron	irons	ironing	ironed	ironed

Verb

① They **iron** their clothes every day.

② My mother **irons** all his shirts.

③ He is not **ironing** his uniform.

④ I **ironed** my pants yesterday morning.

⑤ Why haven't you **ironed** my jacket yet?

Noun

iron • a kind of metal; a household item with a flat base that is heated and used to smooth clothes; any of a series of golf clubs having an iron head

① Is the building reinforced with **iron**?

② My aunt has an electric **iron**.

③ She used a seven **iron** for the shot.

ironing • articles of clothes that have been, or need to be, ironed or pressed; the action of smoothing clothes with a hot iron.

① The **ironing** sat in a basket waiting to be ironed.

② I haven't done my **ironing** for two weeks.

Useful Words and Expressions

iron out • to solve problems or differences

*The two companies tried to **iron out** their problems.*

iron hand • inflexible; very stern; very strict

*He runs his company with an **iron hand**.*

ironing board • a flat surface on which clothes are ironed.

*My **ironing board** is too small.*

too many irons in the fire • to be too busy; not organized

*My friend doesn't have time to study because he has **too many irons in the fire**.*

Now write your own sentences

① iron   • _____

② irons   • _____

③ ironing • _____

④ ironed • _____

⑤ ironed • _____

kill • to cause to die; to put to death; to take life

kill	kills	killing	killed	killed

Verb

① The king threatened to **kill** his servant.

② A lion **kills** to survive.

③ He doesn't like **killing** animals.

④ In America, children are accidentally **killed** by guns every day.

⑤ She says she has never **killed** anything in her life.

Noun

kill • something that has been killed.

The deer was a fresh **kill** from the morning's hunt.

Useful Words and Expressions

dressed to kill • dressed up, often excessively or in poor taste

*His wife was **dressed to kill** at the party last night.*

kill two birds with one stone • to accomplish two goals with one action

*If corporations could solve air pollution and make a profit at the same time, they could **kill two birds with one stone**.*

kill with kindness • to be overly nice or sweet to someone

*Maybe if you **kill him with kindness** he will treat you nicer.*

Now write your own sentences

① **kill** • _____

② **kills** • _____

③ **killing** • _____

④ **killed** • _____

⑤ **killed** • _____

land • to bring an aircraft to the ground; to put into a certain condition or situation

NOTE: The opposite of land (for aircraft) is *take off*

land	lands	landing	landed	landed

Verb

1. Your negative attitude could **land** you in big trouble.
2. If she **lands** the helicopter we'll all be safe.
3. The co-pilot is **landing** the jet.
4. His insider trading **landed** him in jail.
5. I have never **landed** in a blizzard before.

Noun

land • an area of earth; property; real estate

They are going to build a house on their **land** in the country.

Useful Words and Expressions

landlord • a person who rents land or living quarters to others

*My **landlord** is always very nice to me.*

landmark • a very well-known place, location, or monument

*The Statue of Liberty is a very famous **landmark** in America.*

landslide • land, dirt, or mud sliding down from a mountain; to win by a large margin

1. *The **landslide** destroyed the village.*
2. *She won the election by a **landslide**.*

Now write your own sentences

① **land** • _____

② **lands** • _____

③ **landing** • _____

④ **landed** • _____

⑤ **landed** • _____

look • to perform the act of seeing; to use your sight; to make a search of something

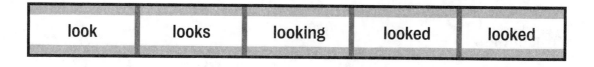

| look | looks | looking | looked | looked |

Verb

① He was so embarrassed he couldn't **look** at her face.
② The principal **looks** at every student's report card.
③ She is **looking** for her coat.
④ Bob **looked** for his lost dog all night long.
⑤ You haven't **looked** in the garage, have you?

Noun

look • the physical appearance of someone or something
 By the **looks** of him I'd say he was very angry.

Useful Words and Expressions

look after • take care of
 *She has to **look after** her aging parents.*
look before you leap • check very carefully before making a decision
 Look before you leap into marriage.
look down on • to have no respect for someone or something; to have contempt for
 *Rich people tend to **look down on** poor people.*
look forward to • excited about the future; anxious about coming events
 *I'm really **looking forward to** the concert.*
look out • a warning of immediate danger
 ***Look out!** There is a snake right next to you.*

lookout • a warning to be alert or careful; someone who watches

   ① *You should always be on the **lookout** for dishonest people in business.*

   ② *He was the **lookout** at the fort.*

look up to • to have respect for; to admire

   *Children need someone to **look up to**.*

Now write your own sentences

① **look** • _____

② **looks** • _____

③ **looking** • _____

④ **looked** • _____

⑤ **looked** • _____

①

Ⓐ He act funny.

Ⓑ She acting funny.

Ⓒ Did he acted funny?

Ⓓ They both acted funny.

②

Ⓐ I couldn't answers the question.

Ⓑ Have you answering the question yet?

Ⓒ My mother couldn't answer the phone.

Ⓓ She did answered it?

③ _____

Ⓐ Please asked her again.

Ⓑ My father ask her.

Ⓒ Did you remember to ask for the money?

Ⓓ I couldn't asks them.

④ _____

Ⓐ Every soldier did attacking last night.

Ⓑ The man attacked her tomorrow.

Ⓒ Did the dog attacks the boy?

Ⓓ Why did you attack him?

⑤ _____

Ⓐ I borrows money every day.

Ⓑ I borrowing it now.

Ⓒ He is borrowing some gas.

Ⓓ Has he borrowing it yet?

⑥ _____

Ⓐ They all helps with the work.

Ⓑ He helped to paint the house.

Ⓒ Have they helping you with your homework?

Ⓓ I can't helps you.

⑦ _____

Ⓐ She has never irons my shirt.

Ⓑ I forgot to ironing my pants.

Ⓒ Didn't you iron my skirt?

Ⓓ He ironing tomorrow.

⑧ _____
     Ⓐ Her child kill the small bird.
     Ⓑ The waitress killed the cockroach.
     Ⓒ Could you kills a deer?
     Ⓓ Next week he killed him.

⑨ _____
     Ⓐ She land plane.
     Ⓑ He landing the plane.
     Ⓒ She landed plane.
     Ⓓ He is landing the plane.

⑩ _____
     Ⓐ You looks nice today.
     Ⓑ You're looked nice today.
     Ⓒ You looking nice today.
     Ⓓ You're looking nice today.

Section IV

Decide whether the underlined word is used as a verb or a noun. Write either <u>V</u> for verb or <u>N</u> for noun for each underlined word in the space after the number.

Example:

① __N__   The first <u>act</u> was very interesting.

② __V__   She can <u>act</u> very well.

① _____   I forgot what the <u>answer</u> was.

② _____   My <u>back</u> really hurts.

③ _____   The <u>bank</u> is closed on Sunday.

④ _____   My roommate's dog <u>barked</u> at the mail carrier.

⑤ _____   She lives on the next <u>block</u>.

⑥ _____ Were there any <u>calls</u> for me?

⑦ _____ Could you <u>check</u> on that information?

⑧ _____ He's a great <u>cook</u>.

⑨ _____ Did you <u>count</u> everyone?

⑩ _____ I went off my <u>diet</u> yesterday.

Section V

Choose the definition that best matches the following useful words and expressions. Write the letter in the space after the number.

Example:

① _A_ acting up   Ⓐ not working right

---

① _____ look out	Ⓐ take care of
② _____ iron hand	Ⓑ a large margin
③ _____ lend a hand	Ⓒ a well-known place
④ _____ count on	Ⓓ a dangerous situation
⑤ _____ look after	Ⓔ a physical exam
⑥ _____ landslide	Ⓕ be careful
⑦ _____ checkup	Ⓖ depend on
⑧ _____ blockbuster	Ⓗ very strict
⑨ _____ over your head	Ⓘ help
⑩ _____ landmark	Ⓙ a great book or movie

mail • to send a letter by postal service or special express

mail	mails	mailing	mailed	mailed

Verb

① "Can you **mail** this package for me, please?"
② My uncle **mails** his daughter a check every month.
③ She is busy **mailing** the letters.
④ I **mailed** everything last weekend.
⑤ Her cousin hasn't **mailed** the gift yet.

Noun

mail • the actual letters, packages, and other parcels sent through the postal system

Did you get any **mail** today?

Useful Words and Expressions

mailing list • list of names and addresses of people who receive certain letters, information, or advertisements

*I wish that company would take me off their **mailing list**.*

mail order • an order that is received and shipped through the postal system

*That **mail order** catalog is really very cheap.*

Now write your own sentences

① **mail** • _____

② **mails** • _____

③ **mailing** • _____

④ **mailed** • _____

⑤ **mailed** • _____

mark • to make a cut, scratch, or scrape on the surface of something; to make an identifying signature, initial or name; to grade school papers; to write down

| mark | marks | marking | marked | marked |

Verb

① Try not to **mark** up the new carpet.

② His cat **marks** all the walls in his apartment.

③ She is **marking** the tests.

④ He couldn't write so he simply **marked** the paper with an X.

⑤ The lazy clerk still hadn't **marked** down the price of the day-old bread.

Noun

mark • a sign, symbol, or signature; a distinguishing sign, scar, stain, blemish, etc., that makes someone or something easy to recognize; the money of Germany

① The artist put her **mark** in the corner of the picture.

② They said the man had a big red **mark** on his cheek.

③ All the tourists exchanged their German **marks** for British pounds.

NOTE: Sometimes the German mark is referred to as the **Deutsche Mark** with a capital **M** in the spelling of mark.

Useful Words and Expressions

make one's mark • to become successful; to become distinguished

*My friend **made her mark** in banking.*

to toe the mark • to work hard; not to quit or give up

*The boss advised everyone **to toe the mark** until the recession was over.*

Now write your own sentences

① **mark**   • _____

② **marks**   • _____

③ **marking** • _____

④ **marked** • _____

⑤ **marked** • _____

market • to offer to buy or sell goods or services

market	markets	marketing	marketed	marketed

Verb

① The scientist wants to **market** her new invention.

② Their trading company **markets** products from China.

③ Her strategy for **marketing** the product made the company a lot of money.

④ Our company aggressively **marketed** the new shoes.

⑤ He had never **marketed** the product outside of his own country.

Noun

market • a place where you can buy things; a grocery store; a supermarket

There is a big **market** close to our house.

Useful Words and Expressions

flea market • an area where people gather to buy, sell, and trade new and used products

*I bought a used pair of jeans at the **flea market**.*

market price • the price for current dealings

*What's the **market price** of a secondhand laptop computer?*

NOTE: Used and secondhand both mean not new. Also, in this meaning, the American spelling of secondhand is one word, not two.

market research • study and research of various trends and conditions in the buying and selling market

*Our **market research** shows that more children are smoking.*

morning market • an area in town where products are sold in the morning

*You can get some good deals at the **morning market**.*

Now write your own sentences

① **market** • _____

② **markets** • _____

③ **marketing** • _____

④ **marketed** • _____

⑤ **marketed** • _____

mind • to pay attention; to obey; to care about or object to

mind	minds	minding	minded	minded

Verb

① Do you **mind** if I smoke?

② John's dog really **minds** well.

③ The child doesn't seem to be **minding** his mother.

④ He **minded** very much what you said.

⑤ Have you ever **minded** flying over the ocean?

Noun

mind • the seat of consciousness; where thought takes place; human reasoning

My **mind** keeps wandering.

Useful Words and Expressions

in the back of one's mind • something that is always being thought of, considered, or remembered

*It was in the **back of his mind** that he might lose his job.*

to have a mind of one's own • to think for yourself; to not be controlled by other people's thinking

*In many cases it is good **to have a mind of your own**.*

out of sight, out of mind • a person or object that is not thought of when not seen for sometime

*When his long lost friend asked why he hadn't written, John replied, "**Out of sight, out of mind**, I guess."*

Now write your own sentences

① mind   • _____

② minds   • _____

③ minding   • _____

④ minded   • _____

⑤ minded   • _____

order • to give a command; to ask for something or someone

order	orders	ordering	ordered	ordered

Verb

① Would you like to **order** dinner now?

② He **orders** everybody around like slaves.

③ I'm **ordering** more office supplies.

④ She **ordered** fish, not steak.

⑤ I have **ordered** already.

Noun

order • in proper arrangement, sequence, or rank; a list of merchandise to be bought or sold

① All the names are in alphabetical **order**.

② She got the biggest sales **order** in company history.

Useful Words and Expressions

in order to • with the purpose of accomplishing something

*We should lower taxes **in order to** give people more spending money.*

in short order • very quickly; taking very little time

*He solved the school's problems **in short order**.*

made-to-order • made according to specific requirements

*You can buy beautiful **made-to-order** suits in Hong Kong.*

out of order • not working properly

*The candy machine is **out of order**.*

Now write your own sentences

① **order**   • _____

② **orders**   • _____

③ **ordering** • _____

④ **ordered**   • _____

⑤ **ordered**   • _____

pack • to fill compactly with things; to fill a suitcase or bag; to load articles into a vehicle

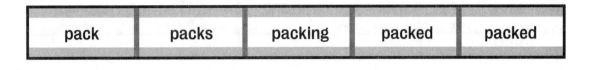

| pack | packs | packing | packed | packed |

Verb

① After we **pack** the car we can go camping.
② When my friend travels, she always **packs** a hair dryer.
③ I'm all done **packing** my suitcase.
④ Everything is **packed**.
⑤ They haven't **packed** yet.

Noun

pack • a group of objects or things grouped together; a group of certain animals that travel together
  ① I'm going to buy a **pack** of chewing gum.
  ② A **pack** of wolves circled the cabin.

Useful Words and Expressions

pack it in • to end or quit something
  *It's starting to rain, so let's **pack it in** and go home.*

Now write your own sentences

① **pack** • _____
② **packs** • _____
③ **packing** • _____
④ **packed** • _____
⑤ **packed** • _____

park • to leave a vehicle in a place for awhile

park	parks	parking	parked	parked

Verb

① I **park** my car in the garage every night.

② Every evening his wife **parks** the tractor in the barn.

③ Sometimes **parking** a car is not easy.

④ I **parked** across the street.

⑤ Have you ever **parked** here before?

Noun

park • a public area for rest and recreation

Let's go to the **park** the day after tomorrow.

Useful Words and Expressions

industrial park • a large area devoted to industry

*Silicon Valley is one huge electronics **industrial park**.*

parking light • a small light on a vehicle used when it is stopped at night

*The truck driver left his **parking lights** on while he slept.*

parking lot • an area where cars are parked

*Every **parking lot** was full.*

parking meter • a coin-operated parking machine

*I forgot to put money in the **parking meter**.*

parking ticket • a notice or ticket given by police for improper parking

*My father got a **parking ticket** this morning.*

Now write your own sentences

① **park** •_____

② **parks** •_____

③ **parking** •_____

④ **parked** •_____

⑤ **parked** •_____

pick • to choose; to make a choice; to decide on something; to detach flowers or fruit

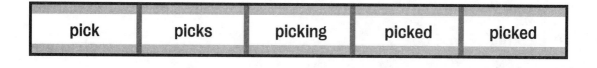

pick	picks	picking	picked	picked

Verb

① They always **pick** the winning horse.
② John **picks** roses every spring from his garden.
③ She's **picking** the new team members tonight.
④ The old man **picked** all the best apples.
⑤ I should have **picked** the corn earlier.

Noun

pick • a heavy, sharp tool used for breaking up rocks or soil

With a **pick** and a shovel she dug her own swimming pool.

Useful Words and Expressions

pick and choose • to select very carefully

*You should **pick and choose** the best words in this book.*

pick on • to tease or make fun of

*The bigger boy keeps **picking on** the smaller children.*

pick out • to choose from a number of people or things

*The victim tried to **pick out** the suspect in the lineup.*

pick up • to meet someone to take along for a ride

*I'm going to **pick up** John at the airport.*

take one's pick • to have the first choice; to have a free choice

*The dog owner said I could **take my pick** of the litter.*

Now write your own sentences

① **pick** • _____

② **picks** • _____

③ **picking** • _____

④ **picked** • _____

⑤ **picked** • _____

plant • to put something in the ground to grow

plant	plants	planting	planted	planted

Verb

① They **plant** flowers every spring and fall.

② The farmer **plants** different crops every year.

③ I love **planting** a vegetable garden.

④ The gentleman farmer **planted** the seeds too late.

⑤ Haven't you ever **planted** tomatoes before?

Noun

plant • fruits, vegetables, and flowers smaller than trees or shrubs; a factory

① All the **plants** in her greenhouse were beautiful.

② The chemical **plant** is on the outskirts of town.

Now write your own sentences

① **plant** • _____

② **plants** • _____

③ **planting** • _____

④ **planted** • _____

⑤ **planted** • _____

play • to take part in a sport or game; to perform on a musical instrument

play	plays	playing	played	played

Verb

① His boss likes to **play** golf.

② My wife **plays** tennis every Sunday.

③ I love **playing** the guitar.

④ They **played** baseball for three hours.

⑤ You haven't **played** cards with us for years.

Noun

play • a performance or stage production

They put on a **play** for charity.

Useful Words and Expressions

play along • to pretend to agree

I **played along** with his idea, but I knew it wouldn't work.

play down • to minimize the importance of something

The suspect tried to **play down** his involvement in the crime.

play dumb • to act ignorantly; to act innocently

If my father asks what happened, just **play dumb**.

play with fire • to take foolish or risky chances

You're **playing with fire** if you don't tell the truth.

play up to • to flatter; to try to win favor with someone

Jim is trying to **play up to** the new girl in the office.

playing cards • cards used for playing card games

There are 52 **playing cards** in a deck.

Now write your own sentences

① play   • _____

② plays   • _____

③ playing   • _____

④ played   • _____

⑤ played   • _____

point • to indicate the position of someone or something, usually with an extended finger

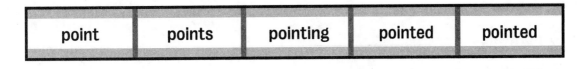

point	points	pointing	pointed	pointed

Verb

① Sometimes children **point** at strangers.
② He **points** in the air when he speaks.
③ The tourists were **pointing** at all the tall buildings.
④ The teacher **pointed** at the clock when the late student arrived.
⑤ I have not **pointed** to anyone yet.

Noun

point • the tip of a tool or weapon; the theme, idea, or concept; an item or detail used to separate a decimal fraction from a whole number; method of keeping score or keeping count

① He sharpened his pencil to a fine **point**.
② That was the most important **point** of her speech.
③ To read 12.6 you say, twelve **point** six.
④ She scored 24 **points** in the basketball game.

Useful Words and Expressions

beside the point • not important; not related to the subject

*Everything you are saying is **beside the point**.*

to get to the point • to be direct

*I wish you would **get to the point** of what you want to say.*

make a point of • to clarify or bring attention to something

*The politician tried to **make a point of** his humble beginnings.*

point out • to identify somebody or something

*The fan tried to **point out** the actor in the crowd.*

Now write your own sentences

① point   • _____

② points   • _____

③ pointing   • _____

④ pointed   • _____

⑤ pointed   • _____

pull • to cause something to move toward oneself; to tear or rip; to drag or tug

pull	pulls	pulling	pulled	pulled

Verb

① Try to **pull** on the rope.

② This new brush **pulls** my hair.

③ The carpenter is **pulling** out all the nails.

④ He was **pulled** to safety by the emergency crew.

⑤ If she hadn't **pulled** him from the river he would have drowned.

Noun

pull • influence or power

Our mayor has a lot of **pull** in Washington, D.C.

Useful Words and Expressions

pull a fast one • to trick or deceive

*He tried to **pull a fast one** by changing his name.*

pull off • to accomplish something; to complete a task

*Do you think she can **pull off** the company merger?*

pull oneself together • to regain control of oneself

*She tried to **pull herself together** after hearing the bad news.*

pull one's punches • to avoid using full force; to speak with restraint

*The outspoken student didn't like to **pull his punches**.*

pull the strings • to have power to do things, usually in a hidden way

*He might be the president but his sister **pulls the strings**.*

pull through • to recover; to get well

*I'm glad she **pulled through** the operation.*

pull together • to work as a group; to work as a team

*If we **pull together**, we can be successful.*

Now write your own sentences

① pull   • _____

② pulls   • _____

③ pulling   • _____

④ pulled   • _____

⑤ pulled   • _____

rent • to take, occupy, or use for a certain time in exchange for money

rent	rents	renting	rented	rented

Verb

① They **rent** a cottage every summer.

② My mother **rents** her house from a friend.

③ Would you consider **renting** an apartment?

④ The man **rented** the car for a week.

⑤ He has **rented** all his life.

Noun

rent • payment from a tenant to the owner or landlord for the use of land or space; money given in return for using something

The **rent** in Tokyo is very expensive.

Useful Words and Expressions

for rent • available to use in return for money

*This condo is **for rent**.*

Now write your own sentences

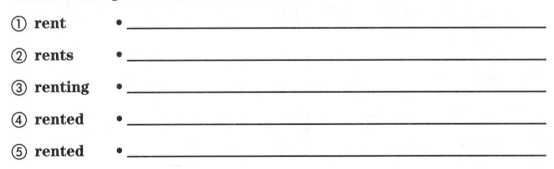

① **rent**   • _____

② **rents**   • _____

③ **renting** • _____

④ **rented** • _____

⑤ **rented** • _____

report • to give an account of something; to tell what happened

report	reports	reporting	reported	reported

Verb

① A reporter's job is to **report** everything she sees.

② The sergeant **reports** all information to his commanding officer.

③ By **reporting** advances in science, doctors can develop new treatments.

④ Our bank manager **reported** the robbery.

⑤ Why haven't you **reported** the missing funds?

Noun

report • a detailed account or statement

The police **report** was false.

Useful Words and Expressions

report back • to give certain information at a later date or time

Report back to me tomorrow evening.

report card • a periodic statement of a student's work or progress

He hesitated to show his report card to his father.

Now write your own sentences

① **report** • _____

② **reports** • _____

③ **reporting** • _____

④ **reported** • _____

⑤ **reported** • _____

rest • to relax or sleep; to relax after a period of activity

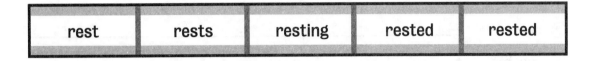

rest	rests	resting	rested	rested

Verb

① Let's **rest** for awhile.

② My dog always **rests** after a long walk.

③ She is **resting** now.

④ I **rested** for about an hour.

⑤ She hasn't **rested** in 48 hours.

Noun

rest • freedom from exertion, work, or worry; remaining part or parts

① You need to take a **rest**.

② Where's the **rest** of your homework?

Useful Words and Expressions

rest home • a place where old or convalescing people can be taken care of

*I never want to live in a **rest home**.*

rest on one's laurels • to rely on past achievements and therefore not work hard to do anything else

*The author wrote one successful book then decided **to rest on his laurels**.*

rest room • toilet; bathroom

*"Could you tell me where the **rest room** is, please?"*

NOTE: The term *rest room* is two words but the term *bathroom* is one word.

final resting place • the location where someone's ashes or body is buried

*I want my **final resting place** to be in the ocean.*

give it a rest • be quiet; quit complaining

*Why don't you **give it a rest** for awhile?*

Now write your own sentences

① **rest** • _____

② **rests** • _____

③ **resting** • _____

④ **rested** • _____

⑤ **rested** • _____

rock • to move gently back and forth; to shake or disturb violently; to surprise with stunning information or breaking news

rock	rocks	rocking	rocked	rocked

Verb
① The boat began to **rock** gently on the waves.
② Every time we have an earthquake it **rocks** our whole building.
③ She is **rocking** the baby to sleep.
④ The stock scandal **rocked** Wall Street.
⑤ News of his resignation has **rocked** the country.

Noun
rock • hard material from the earth's crust; a stone of any size
   The civilians threw **rocks** at the soldiers.

Useful Words and Expressions
rock and roll • a popular type of music originating in the 1950s
   *Elvis made **rock and roll** popular.*
rock bottom • the absolute lowest
   *My **rock bottom** price is $500.*
rock the boat • to cause trouble; to disturb the status quo
   *If you **rock the boat**, you are playing with fire.*
rocking chair • a chair for gently rocking, mounted on rockers
   *John Kennedy used to use a **rocking chair**.*
on the rocks • to order liquor with ice only; heading toward failure
   ① *"I'll have a Scotch **on the rocks**, please."*
   ② *Their marriage is **on the rocks**.*

Now write your own sentences

① **rock**   • _____

② **rocks**   • _____

③ **rocking**   • _____

④ **rocked**   • _____

⑤ **rocked**   • _____

roll • to move in a direction by turning over and over

roll	rolls	rolling	rolled	rolled

Verb

① Try to **roll** the ball into the hole.

② He always **rolls** the bowling ball into the gutter.

③ The workmen are **rolling** the wine barrels out of the warehouse.

④ His dog **rolled** over three times.

⑤ Her daughter had never **rolled** a cigarette before.

Noun

roll • a small piece of bread or pastry

That bakery has great **rolls**.

Useful Words and Expressions

on a roll • having a series of successes; on a winning streak

*Her new company is **on a roll**.*

rolling in dough • to be very rich; to have a lot of money

*Their family's **rolling in dough**.*

rolled into one • to be all combined into one

*With our new loan package, all our debts are **rolled into one**.*

Now write your own sentences

① **roll** • _____

② **rolls** • _____

③ **rolling** • _____

④ **rolled** • _____

⑤ **rolled** • _____

shock • to affect with violent impact; to effect a sudden, disturbing emotion; to receive a large jolt of electricity

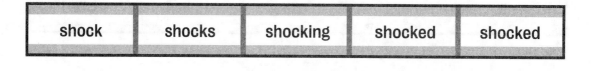

| shock | shocks | shocking | shocked | shocked |

Verb

① The **shock** from the earthquake was felt 700 miles away.
② That teacher **shocks** her students with her straight talk.
③ The electricity kept **shocking** the worker.
④ Mr. Jones was extremely **shocked** when he found out his wife died.
⑤ Had I not moved, I would have been **shocked** by the electric wire.

Noun

shock • a sudden, violent impact that is physical, emotional, or both
    She died of **shock**.

Useful Words and Expressions

shocking pink • a very loud, vibrant shade of pink
    *She loves to wear **shocking pink** dresses.*
sticker shock • the shock a buyer gets when looking at a very expensive sticker price
    *I got **sticker shock** after I looked at the price.*

Now write your own sentences

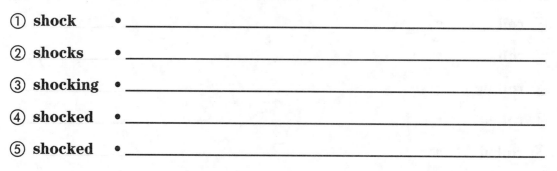

① **shock** • _____
② **shocks** • _____
③ **shocking** • _____
④ **shocked** • _____
⑤ **shocked** • _____

sign • to write your signature; to authorize with a signature

sign	signs	signing	signed	signed

Verb

① I usually **sign** all my company checks.

② My wife **signs** all the invoices.

③ The leaders are **signing** the new trade agreement.

④ He **signed** his initials in a hurry.

⑤ The customer hasn't **signed** his name yet.

Noun

sign • a marker or device to show direction or location; a warning or indication.

① You can see the neon **sign** from a long way off.

② Dark clouds are a **sign** of rain.

Useful Words and Expressions

sign language • a system of communication using visual gestures

*Deaf people use **sign language** to communicate with each other.*

sign of the times • characteristic of the current state of affairs

*It is a **sign of the times** that more people are homeless.*

Now write your own sentences

① **sign** • _____

② **signs** • _____

③ **signing** • _____

④ **signed** • _____

⑤ **signed** • _____

talk • to communicate or exchange ideas or information by spoken word

talk	talks	talking	talked	talked

Verb

1. They **talk** all the time.
2. He **talks** very fast.
3. Are your friends still **talking**?
4. We **talked** all night long.
5. I haven't **talked** to her in five years.

Noun

talk • a speech; a lecture

Professor Miller gave her **talk** on international relations.

Useful Words and Expressions

to know what one is talking about • to be an expert or an authority

*When the lady spoke to the committee, she **knew what she was talking about**.*

now you're talking • to like what someone is saying; to agree with what someone says

Now you're talking when you say let's cut taxes.

talk back • to reply defiantly

*It's not a good idea to **talk back** to the police.*

talk down to • to talk in a superior tone of voice; to speak condescendingly

*He was so arrogant that he **talked down** to everybody.*

talk of the town • what everyone is talking about

*Their new movie is the **talk of the town**.*

talk over • to discuss at length

*Let's **talk over** the business proposal at lunch.*

talk show • a television show where people are interviewed in a question-and-answer format

*Larry King's **talk show** is very popular.*

Now write your own sentences

① **talk** • _____

② **talks** • _____

③ **talking** • _____

④ **talked** • _____

⑤ **talked** • _____

track • to follow the footprints of something or someone; to follow the same path or direction

track	tracks	tracking	tracked	tracked

Verb

① It is very difficult to **track** animals in the wild.
② The new satellite **tracks** all the ships at sea.
③ He's been **tracking** that bear for a week now.
④ The detectives **tracked** him to Las Vegas.
⑤ I still haven't **tracked** down that lost check.

Noun

track • a running course; the footprints left by people or animals

① I took a rest after running around the **track**.
② The tiger's **tracks** led into the jungle.

Useful Words and Expressions

on the right track • to be following the correct procedure, job, or line of reasoning

*I think his niece is **on the right track** with her investigation.*

on the wrong track • to be following the incorrect procedure, job, or line of reasoning

*He got off **on the wrong track** when he accused her of cheating.*

one-track mind • to always think of only one thing

*His relatives have a **one-track mind**—money.*

to be sidetracked • to be diverted from the main subject

*We got **sidetracked** when they all started asking questions at once.*

to lose track of • to fail to follow and keep informed about something or someone

*She was embarrassed that she **lost track of** her checking account.*

to keep track of • to follow and keep informed about something or someone

*Susan was happy that she **kept track of** her high school friends.*

track and field • a group of sports conducted either indoors or outdoors

*Running, pole vault, shot put, long jump and other such sports are included in **track and field**.*

track shoes • shoes specially designed for running on a track

*Recently, **track shoes** have become very expensive.*

Now write your own sentences

① **track** • _____

② **tracks** • _____

③ **tracking** • _____

④ **tracked** • _____

⑤ **tracked** • _____

train

train • to teach; to show or to teach how to do certain things; to get into shape; to prepare for competition

train	trains	training	trained	trained

Verb

① She is going to **train** for the Olympics.

② He **trains** every morning before sunrise.

③ Her aunt is **training** to become a computer operator.

④ My neighbor **trained** his dog to roll over and bark three times.

⑤ They've never **trained** for military service.

Noun

train • a number of railroad cars connected together pulled by an engine; a part of a gown that flows behind the wearer.

① The **train** was almost a mile long.

② Her wedding gown had a long **train.**

Useful Words and Expressions

on-the-job training • learning by doing the actual job; practical, not theoretical, training; hands-on experience

*Many times **on-the-job training** is the quickest way to learn.*

training manual • a book that explains procedures of a company or shows how to work a certain type of machinery

*Make sure you read the **training manual** before you start to work.*

Now write your own sentences

① **train**   •_____

② **trains**   •_____

③ **training**   •_____

④ **trained**   •_____

⑤ **trained**   •_____

travel • to go from one place to another; to take a journey or take a trip

travel	travels	traveling	traveled	traveled

Verb

① My aunt and uncle **travel** to the Caribbean every winter.

② Her father **travels** to New York three times a week.

③ Our doctor is **traveling** to Paris tomorrow.

④ When I was young I **traveled** a lot.

⑤ His grandmother has never **traveled** abroad.

Useful Words and Expressions

travel agent • a person who makes travel arrangements

   *Their **travel agent** was really helpful.*

travel agency • a company that makes travel arrangements

   *That **travel agency** isn't cheap.*

traveling companion • a person who travels with another person, sometimes for pay

   *My grandfather is looking for a **traveling companion**.*

well-traveled • to have experience in traveling

   *The mayor was very **well-traveled**.*

Now write your own sentences

① **travel** • _____

② **travels** • _____

③ **traveling** • _____

④ **traveled** • _____

⑤ **traveled** • _____

turn • to move around an axis or center; to make a rotating motion to change direction

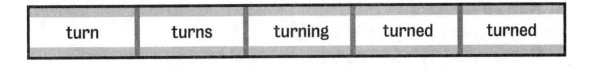

turn	turns	turning	turned	turned

Verb

① "Can you **turn** right at the next corner, please?"
② The steering wheel **turns** very easily.
③ All the gears are **turning** in opposite directions.
④ We **turned** off the main road and rested for awhile.
⑤ Had she not **turned** we would have had an accident.

Noun

turn • a change in direction; position in a successive order

    ① Take the next **turn** off the highway.
    ② Whose **turn** is it?

Useful Words and Expressions

take turns • to alternate back and forth
    *In baseball, both teams **take turns** batting.*
turn back • to go back in the opposite direction
    *We decided to **turn back** when we ran out of water.*
turn down • to refuse; to decrease the sound or volume
    ① *My company **turned down** my request for a transfer.*
    ② ***Turn down** the TV.*
turn in • to hand something in; to go to bed
    ① *Please **turn in** your report next Monday.*
    ② *I think I'll **turn in** early tonight.*

turn off • to stop the flow of something, such as water, gas, or electricity

Turn off the stove.

turn on • to start the flow of something, such as water, gas, or electricity

Turn on the lights.

turn one's back on • to abandon or ignore

The angry father turned his back on his son.

turnout • the number of people in attendance

The turnout for the conference was very high.

turnover • amount of business done at a given time; the number of workers who leave a company

① *The company's business turnover is more than expected.*

② *Their employee turnover is lower than normal.*

turn the tables • to change positions, usually from an inferior to a superior position

The underdog team turned the tables and won the game.

turn up • to arrive or show up; to discover something; to increase the sound or volume

① *Her date never turned up.*

② *The investigation turned up new evidence.*

③ *Can you turn up the radio, please?*

Now write your own sentences

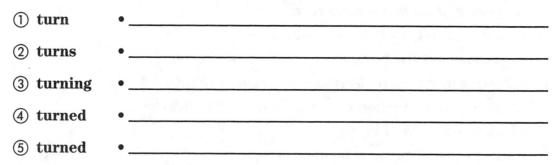

① **turn** • _____

② **turns** • _____

③ **turning** • _____

④ **turned** • _____

⑤ **turned** • _____

walk • to move on foot; to go places on foot at a moderate pace

walk	walks	walking	walked	walked

Verb

① I **walk** to school everyday.

② She **walks** to town every other Saturday.

③ He hates **walking** in the rain.

④ The man **walked** very slowly along the path.

⑤ Some people have never **walked** to work.

Noun

walk • an excursion on foot; a place for walking

① Let's go for a **walk**.

② They strolled along the **walk**.

Useful Words and Expressions

walk away with • to win a prize

*His sister **walked away with** first prize.*

walk-on • a person who shows up, usually uninvited, to try out for a competition

*He is the **walk-on** that got signed to the team.*

walk out • to go on strike

*The union decided to **walk out** on Friday.*

walk out on • to abandon or desert someone

*She was shocked when her husband **walked out on** her.*

Now write your own sentences

① walk • _____

② walks • _____

③ walking • _____

④ walked • _____

⑤ walked • _____

water • to moisten or supply plants and animals with water

water	waters	watering	watered	watered

Verb

① My little sister loves to **water** the lawn.

② His wife **waters** her garden once a day.

③ I'm **watering** the plants.

④ After the long ride the cowboy **watered** the horses.

⑤ He hasn't **watered** the livestock.

Noun

water • a transparent liquid that makes up rain, oceans, rivers and lakes

The **water** in the river was ice cold.

Useful Words and Expressions

hot water • trouble; bad situation

*He got into **hot water** when he came home late last night.*

watercolor • pigment based in water as opposed to oil

*She uses **watercolor** extensively in her paintings.*

watercooler • a device for cooling water for drinking

*They bought a brand new **watercooler** for the office.*

to water down • to make weaker; to dilute

① *The new law is so **watered down** that it is useless.*

② *This drink tastes like it has been **watered down**.*

waterfall • a steep fall of water from a high place

*Angel Falls in Argentina is the highest **waterfall** in the world.*

water glass • a drinking glass meant to hold water

*There was a **water glass** and a wine glass on the table.*

watermelon • a large, round, green melon with red, juicy fruit inside

*I used to go **watermelon** picking every summer.*

waterproof • protected from the penetration of water

*My rain boots are **waterproof**.*

water-repellent • somewhat protected from water but not entirely waterproof

*That fishing vest is **water-repellent**.*

waterskiing • gliding over water on skis while being pulled by a boat

***Waterskiing** is not as easy as it looks.*

Now write your own sentences

① **water** • _____

② **waters** • _____

③ **watering** • _____

④ **watered** • _____

⑤ **watered** • _____

work • to engage in physical or mental activity; to do physical labor; to perform physically or mentally for pay

work	works	working	worked	worked

Verb

① Believe it or not, I **work** 16 hours a day.

② His father **works** in a factory.

③ My daughter's going to be **working** during spring break.

④ Her boyfriend **worked** part-time after school.

⑤ Have you **worked** in the garden today?

Noun

work • a job, employment, or occupation

He got fired last week, so now he is looking for **work**.

Useful Words and Expressions

work on • to try to solve a problem

*Let's **work on** it until we figure out the answer.*

work out • to try to solve a problem; to do strenuous physical exercise

① *I hope we can **work out** our differences.*

② *She loves to **work out** at the gym.*

work up • to generate excitement

*The band tried to **work up** the crowd by playing very loud music.*

workable • capable of doing or putting into practice

*I think her idea is very **workable**.*

workaholic • a person who works obsessively; a person who works all the time and takes no vacations

*Some people accuse me of being a **workaholic**.*

work around • to work around something or someone difficult

*He's in a bad mood, so try to **work around** him today.*

workbench • table where a craftsman works

*My wife built her own **workbench** in our garage.*

workbook • a book containing questions, exercises, and tests to help students learn

*This **workbook** will help you learn a lot of new words.*

Now write your own sentences

① **work** • _____

② **works** • _____

③ **working** • _____

④ **worked** • _____

⑤ **worked** • _____

Comprehensive Test #1

PURE REGULAR VERBS

Student Name _____

Student Number _____

Score _____ / ___50___

Directions: This is a timed test. Follow the instructions for each section. There are 50 questions worth one point each.

Section I

> Choose the definition that best matches the verb. Write the letter in the space after the number.
>
> **Example:**
>
> ① __A__ act   Ⓐ perform in a play

① _____ block   Ⓐ reply to a question

② _____ pick   Ⓑ prepare food

③ _____ rest   Ⓒ communicate ideas

④ _____ travel   Ⓓ do physical labor

⑤ _____ answer   Ⓔ grade school papers

⑥ _____ walk   Ⓕ stop someone or something

⑦ _____ mark   Ⓖ move on foot

⑧ _____ work   Ⓗ take a trip

⑨ _____ talk   Ⓘ choose

⑩ _____ cook   Ⓙ relax

Section II

Write the correct verb tense in the blank space. All verbs must be
spelled correctly.

Example:

① I <u>mailed</u> the letter yesterday.   (mail)

① She is _____ the question.   (answer)

② I'm _____ all the equipment.   (check)

③ They _____ up north last night.   (head)

④ He has never _____ an animal.   (kill)

⑤ Their plane hasn't _____ yet.   (land)

⑥ When are you going to be _____ the letter?   (mail)

⑦ She is _____ the new product overseas.   (market)

⑧ My father hasn't _____ golf in years.   (play)

⑨ I had to _____ last night.   (work)

⑩ He is _____ the lawn.   (water)

Section III

Decide which sentence is correct. Write the letter in the space after the
number.

Example:

① __C__

     Ⓐ He look out the window.

     Ⓑ They looking around now.

     Ⓒ She looked at the picture and smiled.

     Ⓓ Looks at that red sports car!

①

Ⓐ He answer question.

Ⓑ He answered question.

Ⓒ He answered the question.

Ⓓ He's answered question.

② ____

Ⓐ She blocking shot.

Ⓑ The police blocking exit.

Ⓒ His car blocked the driveway.

Ⓓ He block him.

③ ____

Ⓐ She's checking the time.

Ⓑ They checked it tomorrow.

Ⓒ I'm checks the list.

Ⓓ He check it yesterday.

④ ____

Ⓐ Remember to duck.

Ⓑ I ducks under the doorway.

Ⓒ They did ducked.

Ⓓ He duckings under it.

⑤ ____

Ⓐ The hunter kill lion.

Ⓑ They had to kill the horse.

Ⓒ We had to killed the dog.

Ⓓ We kills it.

⑥

Ⓐ Have you mailing it yet?

Ⓑ Did you have mailing it?

Ⓒ I have mailed it.

Ⓓ I have mail it.

⑦ _____

  Ⓐ I'm renting an apartment.
  Ⓑ She rent apartment.
  Ⓒ Do you renting?
  Ⓓ Would you rents an apartment?

⑧ _____

  Ⓐ They picking that one.
  Ⓑ I haven't picks it yet.
  Ⓒ You can pick any one.
  Ⓓ She'll picked that one.

⑨ _____

  Ⓐ Please sign here.
  Ⓑ Signs here, please.
  Ⓒ You would signs here please.
  Ⓓ Please signing here.

⑩ _____

  Ⓐ Do you works very hard?
  Ⓑ Has he worked hard?
  Ⓒ Does they work hard?
  Ⓓ Didn't she working hard?

Section IV

> Decide whether the underlined word is used as a verb or a noun. Write either <u>V</u> for verb or <u>N</u> for noun for each underlined word in the space after the number.
>
> **Example:**
> ① __N__   The first <u>act</u> was very interesting.
> ② __V__   She can <u>act</u> very well.

① _____   I'm going to <u>answer</u>.

② _____   She had a heart <u>attack</u>.

③ ____   I'll <u>back</u> your idea in the meeting.

④ ____   He wrote me a <u>check</u>.

⑤ ____   Let's take a <u>rest</u>.

⑥ ____   He threw a <u>rock</u>.

⑦ ____   I hate my <u>work</u>.

⑧ ____   She wants to <u>train</u> very hard.

⑨ ____   Shall we go for a <u>walk</u>?

⑩ ____   Do you have some <u>water</u>?

Section V

Choose the definition that best matches the following useful words and expressions. Write the letter in the space after the number.

Example:

① __A__ acting up   Ⓐ not working right

① ____ play up to   Ⓐ complete a task

② ____ rest room   Ⓑ the absolute lowest

③ ____ on a roll   Ⓒ learning by doing

④ ____ talk over   Ⓓ in trouble

⑤ ____ one-track mind   Ⓔ solve a problem

⑥ ____ in hot water   Ⓕ discuss at length

⑦ ____ rock bottom   Ⓖ toilet; bathroom

⑧ ____ iron out   Ⓗ a winning streak

⑨ ____ on-the-job training   Ⓘ thinking of one thing

⑩ ____ pull off   Ⓙ flatter

Comprehensive Test #2

PURE REGULAR VERBS

Student Name _____

Student Number _____

Score _____ / __50__

> **Directions:** This is a timed test. Follow the instructions for each section. There are 50 questions worth one point each.

Section I

> Choose the definition that best matches the verb. Write the letter in the space after the number.
>
> **Example:**
> ① __A__ act   Ⓐ perform

① _____ ask	Ⓐ get a loan
② _____ count	Ⓑ eat special food
③ _____ market	Ⓒ smooth with a hot object
④ _____ borrow	Ⓓ put into the ground to grow
⑤ _____ pull	Ⓔ give plants or animals water
⑥ _____ rock	Ⓕ drag or tug
⑦ _____ water	Ⓖ state a question
⑧ _____ plant	Ⓗ offer to buy or sell
⑨ _____ iron	Ⓘ shake or disturb
⑩ _____ diet	Ⓙ use numbers

Section II

Write the correct verb tense in the blank space. All verbs must be spelled correctly.

Example:

① I <u>mailed</u> the letter yesterday.   (mail)

① The teacher has _____ to school every day.   (walk)

② He hasn't _____ yet.   (order)

③ Have you started _____ for the trip?   (pack)

④ The bear is going to _____ the hunter.   (attack)

⑤ I want to _____ half my check every month.   (bank)

⑥ She said she wasn't going to _____ my idea.   (back)

⑦ The tall man didn't _____ in time.   (duck)

⑧ My father has never _____ from a bank.   (borrow)

⑨ Who are you _____ ?   (call)

⑩ I wish that dog would quit _____ .   (bark)

Section III

Decide which sentence is correct. Write the letter in the space after the number.

Example:

① __C__

Ⓐ He look out the window.

Ⓑ They looking around now.

Ⓒ She looked at the picture and smiled.

Ⓓ Looks at that red sports car!

① _____

Ⓐ They acts happy.

Ⓑ She acted very quickly.

Ⓒ My mother didn't acting.

Ⓓ He hadn't acts before.

② _____

Ⓐ I had asks her.

Ⓑ Had you asking him already?

Ⓒ The child asked us.

Ⓓ You didn't have asks them?

③ _____

Ⓐ He called me tomorrow.

Ⓑ I'm called her.

Ⓒ Can you called later?

Ⓓ They haven't called yet?

④ _____

Ⓐ I cook breakfast.

Ⓑ They cooks breakfast.

Ⓒ Didn't she cooking breakfast?

Ⓓ He cooked breakfast tomorrow.

⑤ _____

Ⓐ They heading school.

Ⓑ They are heading school.

Ⓒ They headed school.

Ⓓ They are heading for school.

⑥ _____

Ⓐ The plane landing safely.

Ⓑ The plane hasn't landed yet.

Ⓒ Hasn't the plane landing?

Ⓓ Did the plane landed?

⑦ ____
    Ⓐ Park the car in the garage.
    Ⓑ Please parked the car in the garage.
    Ⓒ Can you parking the car in the garage?
    Ⓓ Did you parked the car?

⑧ ____
    Ⓐ I like to play tennis.
    Ⓑ Do you like to playing tennis?
    Ⓒ Does she like played tennis?
    Ⓓ Have you ever play tennis?

⑨ ____
    Ⓐ They are always talks.
    Ⓑ He never talks.
    Ⓒ She hardly ever talking.
    Ⓓ Don't you talked?

⑩ ____
    Ⓐ He is watered the lawn.
    Ⓑ He did watering the lawn.
    Ⓒ Did he water the lawn?
    Ⓓ He didn't watered the lawn.

Section IV

Decide whether the underlined word is used as a verb or a noun. Write either <u>V</u> for verb or <u>N</u> for noun for each underlined word in the space after the number.

Example:

① __N__   The first <u>act</u> was very interesting.

② __V__   She can <u>act</u> very well.

① ____   I'm going to <u>bank</u> this check tomorrow.

② ____   We live on the same <u>block</u>.

DOUGLAS COLLEGE LIBRARIES

③ _____   He isn't a good <u>cook</u>.

④ _____   The <u>cover</u> is made of plastic.

⑤ _____   Do you want a <u>roll</u> with your coffee?

⑥ _____   Did you <u>sign</u> your name?

⑦ _____   Can you <u>talk</u> to her?

⑧ _____   Do you <u>travel</u> a lot?

⑨ _____   Take the next <u>turn</u>.

⑩ _____   Don't forget your <u>pack</u>.

Section V

> Choose the definition that best matches the following useful words and expressions. Write the letter in the space after the number.
>
> **Example:**
> ① __A__ acting up   Ⓐ not working right

① _____ look forward to   Ⓐ cancel or stop

② _____ pick on   Ⓑ choose one from many

③ _____ get to the point   Ⓒ not important

④ _____ rock the boat   Ⓓ agree with

⑤ _____ in short order   Ⓔ solve a problem

⑥ _____ pick out   Ⓕ be direct

⑦ _____ now you're talking   Ⓖ make fun of

⑧ _____ work out   Ⓗ be excited about the future

⑨ _____ beside the point   Ⓘ cause trouble

⑩ _____ call off   Ⓙ very quickly

Comprehensive Test #3

PURE REGULAR VERBS

Student Name _____

Student Number _____

Score _____ / ____50____

Directions: This is a timed test. Follow the instructions for each section. There are 50 questions worth one point each.

Section I

Choose the definition that best matches the verb. Write the letter in the space after the number.

Example:

1. __A__ act   Ⓐ perform

---

① _____ attack	Ⓐ make a mark
② _____ back	Ⓑ follow a story
③ _____ hand	Ⓒ go in a certain direction
④ _____ play	Ⓓ turn over and over
⑤ _____ shock	Ⓔ write your signature
⑥ _____ check	Ⓕ affect with violent impact
⑦ _____ roll	Ⓖ take part in sports
⑧ _____ head	Ⓗ give directly
⑨ _____ cover	Ⓘ try to kill something
⑩ _____ sign	Ⓙ return

Section II

Write the correct verb tense in the blank space. All verbs must be spelled correctly.

Example:

① I <u>mailed</u> the letter yesterday.   (mail)

① The player couldn't _____ the kick.   (block)

② I will have _____ dinner by that time.   (cook)

③ The boss is _____ on you to help.   (count)

④ She will be _____ over the papers tomorrow.   (hand)

⑤ His aunt would always _____ for a long time.   (talk)

⑥ Her young son is _____ mud into the house.   (track)

⑦ He will be _____ his dog not to bark.   (train)

⑧ We couldn't _____ the old tree out.   (pull)

⑨ My mother cannot _____ now.   (rest)

⑩ They're _____ around the world.   (travel)

Section III

Decide which sentence is correct. Write the letter in the space after the number.

Example:

① _C_

Ⓐ He look out the window.

Ⓑ They looking around now.

Ⓒ She looked at the picture and smiled.

Ⓓ Looks at that red sports car!

① _____
- Ⓐ She walk to work.
- Ⓑ I walks to my job.
- Ⓒ They both walked together.
- Ⓓ Hadn't they walking?

② _____
- Ⓐ We travels alone.
- Ⓑ They traveling to Europe.
- Ⓒ When have you traveling?
- Ⓓ Do you often travel?

③ _____
- Ⓐ I'm look for a new apartment.
- Ⓑ She's looking for a used car.
- Ⓒ I'll be looked tomorrow.
- Ⓓ Don't you looked?

④ _____
- Ⓐ He ironing tomorrow.
- Ⓑ She ironed it this morning.
- Ⓒ They irons every night.
- Ⓓ My mother ironing.

⑤ _____
- Ⓐ She diet every year.
- Ⓑ Dieting is good for you.
- Ⓒ They dieting now.
- Ⓓ Didn't they dieted?

⑥ _____
- Ⓐ Can I borrows it?
- Ⓑ I couldn't borrowed any money.
- Ⓒ She borrowing it yesterday.
- Ⓓ I've never borrowed anything.

⑦ _____
- Ⓐ The dog barked tomorrow.
- Ⓑ Her dog keeps barked.
- Ⓒ The police officer barked out orders.
- Ⓓ It bark now.

⑧ ____
    Ⓐ Please helps me.
    Ⓑ He is helped them.
    Ⓒ She couldn't help it.
    Ⓓ Did they helping?

⑨ ____
    Ⓐ He turn here.
    Ⓑ They have turning.
    Ⓒ Please turn here.
    Ⓓ I turns there.

⑩ ____
    Ⓐ Please pulls it harder.
    Ⓑ I'm not pulled the rope.
    Ⓒ Haven't you pulling the rope?
    Ⓓ Why haven't you pulled the rope?

Section IV

Decide whether the underlined word is used as a verb or a noun. Write either <u>V</u> for verb or <u>N</u> for noun for each underlined word in the space after the number.

Example:

① __N__   The first <u>act</u> was very interesting.
② __V__   She can <u>act</u> very well.

① ____   I don't want to <u>rent</u>.

② ____   She has a lot of <u>pull</u>.

③ ____   Don't <u>track</u> dirt into the house.

④ ____   I've never gotten over the <u>shock</u>.

⑤ ____   Don't <u>point</u>.

⑥ ____   Are you ready to <u>order</u>?

⑦ ____   Do you <u>mind</u> helping?

⑧ ____   Any <u>mail</u> for me?

⑨ ____   How did you like the <u>play</u>?

⑩ ____   Can you <u>market</u> this product?

Section V

> Choose the definition that best matches the following useful words and
> expressions. Write the letter in the space after the number.
>
> **Example:**
> ① _A_ acting up   Ⓐ not working right

① get your act together   Ⓐ message machine

② blockbuster   Ⓑ trying to start trouble

③ count on   Ⓒ be grateful

④ duck out   Ⓓ protect yourself

⑤ give a hand to   Ⓔ famous site

⑥ landmark   Ⓕ a great book or movie

⑦ asking for it   Ⓖ applaud

⑧ count your blessings   Ⓗ depend on

⑨ cover yourself   Ⓘ get organized

⑩ answering machine   Ⓙ leave quickly; hide

Comprehensive Test #4

PURE REGULAR VERBS

Student Name _____

Student Number _____

Score _____ / ___50___

Directions: This is a timed test. Follow the instructions for each section. There are 50 questions worth one point each.

Section I

Choose the definition that best matches the verb. Write the letter in the space after the number.

Example:

① _A_ act   Ⓐ perform

---

① _____ track   Ⓐ a dog does this
② _____ call   Ⓑ opposite of takeoff
③ _____ help   Ⓒ fill a suitcase
④ _____ order   Ⓓ leave a car for awhile
⑤ _____ pack   Ⓔ deposit money
⑥ _____ bark   Ⓕ use in exchange for money
⑦ _____ bank   Ⓖ follow footprints
⑧ _____ land   Ⓗ give a command
⑨ _____ rent   Ⓘ phone someone
⑩ _____ park   Ⓙ give support

Section II

Write the correct verb tense in the blank space. All verbs must be
spelled correctly.

Example:

① I <u>mailed</u> the letter yesterday.   (mail)

① He was _____ very strangely.   (act)

② I've been _____ for six months.   (diet)

③ They have never offered to _____.   (help)

④ Her parents _____ a cottage last summer.   (rent)

⑤ Last night's earthquake _____ the house.   (rock)

⑥ I hate to _____ clothes.   (iron)

⑦ Why don't you _____ him?   (ask)

⑧ She _____ her motorcycle every evening.   (cover)

⑨ He _____ around before he went inside.   (look)

⑩ When I called he didn't _____ around.   (turn)

Section III

Decide which sentence is correct. Write the letter in the space after the
number.

Example:

① __C__

Ⓐ He look out the window.

Ⓑ They looking around now.

Ⓒ She looked at the picture and smiled.

Ⓓ Looks at that red sports car!

①

Ⓐ Could you hands me that paper?

Ⓑ Tomorrow they will hands it over.

Ⓒ She had already handed it to them.

Ⓓ Can she handing it to them?

② _____

Ⓐ Please covers the machine.

Ⓑ He usually covers his bike at night.

Ⓒ He usually covering his bike.

Ⓓ Doesn't he usually covering his bike?

③ _____

Ⓐ I'm count on you.

Ⓑ They counts on her for help.

Ⓒ I can't count on them.

Ⓓ He count on them.

④ _____

Ⓐ Let's go backs home now.

Ⓑ He not backed the plan.

Ⓒ They all backed her up.

Ⓓ Do you backs the new idea?

⑤ _____

Ⓐ He roll ball.

Ⓑ He rolling the ball.

Ⓒ He rolled the ball.

Ⓓ He rolling ball.

⑥ _____

Ⓐ Let's resting for awhile.

Ⓑ Let's resting.

Ⓒ Let's rest.

Ⓓ Let's rested for awhile.

⑦ _____

Ⓐ We were all shock.

Ⓑ They were all shocked.

Ⓒ They were shocking by the news.

Ⓓ They were shocks about the story.

⑧ ____
      Ⓐ The boy tracked dirt into the house.
      Ⓑ To tracked the tiger was difficult.
      Ⓒ The police are tracked the criminals.
      Ⓓ The hunter will tracking the animal.

⑨ ____
      Ⓐ Can you train my dog?
      Ⓑ I can't trains him.
      Ⓒ I can't training him.
      Ⓓ I can't trained him.

⑩ ____
      Ⓐ Our father is points his finger.
      Ⓑ My mother is pointed her finger.
      Ⓒ His sister was points her finger.
      Ⓓ They all pointed their fingers.

Section IV

Decide whether the underlined word is used as a verb or a noun. Write either <u>V</u> for verb or <u>N</u> for noun for each underlined word in the space after the number.

Example:

①   N   The first <u>act</u> was very interesting.
②   V   She can <u>act</u> very well.

① ____   Please <u>count</u> to 100.

② ____   I never <u>diet</u> for very long.

③ ____   He didn't <u>duck</u> in time.

④ ____   She hit her <u>head</u>.

⑤ ____   Did you buy some <u>land</u>?

⑥ ____   Can you <u>help</u>?

⑦ _____   He gave me a strange <u>look</u>.

⑧ _____   The gate was made of <u>iron</u>.

⑨ _____   Would you <u>hand</u> me that?

⑩ _____   When will you <u>plant</u> it?

Section V

Choose the definition that best matches the following useful words and expressions. Write the letter in the space after the number.

Example:
① __A__ acting up   Ⓐ not working right

① _____ landlord   Ⓐ depending on someone

② _____ pack it in   Ⓑ not working properly

③ _____ parking lot   Ⓒ take risky chances

④ _____ walk away with   Ⓓ trick or deceive

⑤ _____ back down   Ⓔ abandon or desert

⑥ _____ banking on   Ⓕ end or quit

⑦ _____ play with fire   Ⓖ admit defeat

⑧ _____ walk out on   Ⓗ win a prize

⑨ _____ pull a fast one   Ⓘ landowner

⑩ _____ out of order   Ⓙ place to park cars

Comprehensive Test #5

PURE REGULAR VERBS

Student Name _____

Student Number _____

Score _____ / ___50___

> **Directions:** This is a timed test. Follow the instructions for each section. There are 50 questions worth one point each.

Section I

> Choose the definition that best matches the verb. Write the letter in the space after the number.
>
> **Example:**
> ① __A__ act   Ⓐ perform

① _____ duck	Ⓐ pretend in form or manner
② _____ look	Ⓑ cause to die
③ _____ mail	Ⓒ show with a finger
④ _____ report	Ⓓ teach; show
⑤ _____ turn	Ⓔ quickly get down
⑥ _____ train	Ⓕ change direction
⑦ _____ point	Ⓖ pay attention
⑧ _____ act	Ⓗ tell what happened
⑨ _____ kill	Ⓘ send a letter
⑩ _____ mind	Ⓙ perform the act of seeing

Section II

Write the correct verb tense in the blank space. All verbs must be spelled correctly.

Example:

① I <u>mailed</u> the letter yesterday.   (mail)

① Make sure to _____ it fragile.   (mark)

② The naughty child never has _____ his parents.   (mind)

③ I was _____ the car in the parking lot.   (park)

④ The sound of thunder came _____ down the valley.   (roll)

⑤ Her story didn't _____ anybody.   (shock)

⑥ The customer forgot to _____ the check.   (sign)

⑦ He would always _____ his finger at people.   (point)

⑧ No damages were _____ .   (report)

⑨ Can you help her _____ out a new suit?   (pick)

⑩ We're going to _____ some roses this spring.   (plant)

Section III

Decide which sentence is correct. Write the letter in the space after the number.

Example:

① _C_

Ⓐ He look out the window.

Ⓑ They looking around now.

Ⓒ She looked at the picture and smiled.

Ⓓ Looks at that red sports car!

① _____
  Ⓐ He's banked there for years.
  Ⓑ She bank there for 10 years.
  Ⓒ Have you always banking here?
  Ⓓ Haven't you ever banking anywhere else?

② _____
  Ⓐ The earthquake rock our house.
  Ⓑ Didn't the earthquake rock your house?
  Ⓒ Hasn't the earthquake rocking your house?
  Ⓓ The earthquake hasn't rocks our house

③ _____
  Ⓐ Let's plant a garden this fall.
  Ⓑ Let's planting a garden this spring.
  Ⓒ Do you plants a garden this summer?
  Ⓓ Have you ever plants winter garden?

④ _____
  Ⓐ My suitcase is packs.
  Ⓑ My suitcase isn't packs.
  Ⓒ He pack his suitcase.
  Ⓓ He packs his suitcase.

⑤ _____
  Ⓐ Can you orders for me?
  Ⓑ I have not yet ordering.
  Ⓒ I have not ordered.
  Ⓓ Have you ordering yet?

⑥ _____
  Ⓐ The child doesn't minding.
  Ⓑ I wish he had minded his mother.
  Ⓒ Did you minds when you were a child?
  Ⓓ He never minding when he was young.

⑦ _____
  Ⓐ He's marketing a new idea.
  Ⓑ He market a new idea.
  Ⓒ She was marketed a new idea.
  Ⓓ Did you marketing a new idea?

⑧ _____
 Ⓐ Did you marks the papers?
 Ⓑ He didn't marked his papers.
 Ⓒ She forgot to mark her papers.
 Ⓓ Hadn't they marks the papers.

⑨ _____
 Ⓐ Can you reporting?
 Ⓑ I did reported last evening.
 Ⓒ You should report it to the police.
 Ⓓ I'll reported it tomorrow.

⑩ _____
 Ⓐ Nobody help.
 Ⓑ Nobody helped.
 Ⓒ Is nobody help?
 Ⓓ Has nobody helping?

Section IV

Decide whether the underlined word is used as a verb or a noun. Write either <u>V</u> for verb or <u>N</u> for noun for each underlined word in the space after the number.

Example:
① __N__ The first <u>act</u> was very interesting.
② __V__ She can <u>act</u> very well.

① _____ I have a <u>pick</u> and a shovel.

② _____ <u>Park</u> it here.

③ _____ They didn't <u>mark</u> it very well.

④ _____ The second <u>act</u> was terrible.

⑤ _____ There's a <u>call</u> for you.

⑥ _____ Why do you <u>ask</u>?

⑦ ____ He wants to <u>kill</u> the idea.

⑧ ____ The <u>bark</u> on the tree was very thick.

⑨ ____ Did you see the <u>sign</u>?

⑩ ____ I forgot to <u>look</u>.

Section V

Choose the definition that best matches the following useful words and expressions. Write the letter in the space after the number.

Example:

① _A_ acting up   Ⓐ not working right

① ____ checkbook

② ____ head cold

③ ____ landslide

④ ____ cover-up

⑤ ____ living on borrowed time

⑥ ____ parking meter

⑦ ____ flea market

⑧ ____ give a helping hand

⑨ ____ check in

⑩ ____ play along

Ⓐ be in serious trouble

Ⓑ plan for hiding the truth

Ⓒ lend support

Ⓓ register

Ⓔ place where things are bought and sold

Ⓕ a book that holds checks

Ⓖ pretend to agree

Ⓗ a common cold

Ⓘ coin-operated parking machine

Ⓙ a large margin

Midterm Test Answer Key

Section I	Section II	Section III	Section IV	Section V
1. G	1. answer	1. D	1. N	1. F
2. J	2. barking	2. C	2. N	2. H
3. I	3. blocking	3. C	3. N	3. I
4. H	4. cover	4. D	4. V	4. G
5. A	5. asked	5. C	5. N	5. A
6. C	6. counted	6. B	6. N	6. B
7. D	7. dieted	7. C	7. V	7. E
8. E	8. head	8. B	8. N	8. J
9. F	9. cooked	9. D	9. V	9. D
10. B	10. bank	10. D	10. N	10. C

Comprehensive Test #1 Answer Key

Section I	Section II	Section III	Section IV	Section V
1. F	1. answering	1. C	1. V	1. J
2. I	2. checking	2. C	2. N	2. G
3. J	3. headed	3. A	3. V	3. H
4. H	4. killed	4. A	4. N	4. F
5. A	5. landed	5. B	5. N	5. I
6. G	6. mailing	6. C	6. N	6. D
7. E	7. marketing	7. A	7. N	7. B
8. D	8. played	8. C	8. V	8. E
9. C	9. work	9. A	9. N	9. C
10. B	10. watering	10. B	10. N	10. A

Comprehensive Test #2 Answer Key

Section I	Section II	Section III	Section IV	Section V
1. G	1. walked	1. B	1. V	1. H
2. J	2. ordered	2. C	2. N	2. G
3. H	3. packing	3. D	3. N	3. F
4. A	4. attack	4. A	4. N	4. I
5. F	5. bank	5. D	5. N	5. J
6. I	6. back	6. B	6. V	6. B
7. E	7. duck	7. A	7. V	7. D
8. D	8. borrowed	8. A	8. V	8. E
9. C	9. calling	9. B	9. N	9. C
10. B	10. barking	10. C	10. N	10. A

Comprehensive Test #3 Answer Key

Section I	Section II	Section III	Section IV	Section V
1. I	1. block	1. C	1. V	1. I
2. J	2. cooked	2. D	2. N	2. F
3. H	3. counting	3. B	3. V	3. H
4. G	4. handing	4. B	4. N	4. J
5. F	5. talk	5. B	5. V	5. G
6. A	6. tracking	6. D	6. V	6. E
7. D	7. training	7. C	7. V	7. B
8. C	8. pull	8. C	8. N	8. C
9. B	9. rest	9. C	9. N	9. D
10. E	10. traveling	10. D	10. V	10. A

Comprehensive Test #4 Answer Key

Section I	Section II	Section III	Section IV	Section V
1. G	1. acting	1. C	1. V	1. I
2. I	2. dieting	2. B	2. V	2. F
3. J	3. help	3. C	3. V	3. J
4. H	4. rented	4. C	4. N	4. H
5. C	5. rocked	5. C	5. N	5. G
6. A	6. iron	6. C	6. V	6. A
7. E	7. ask	7. B	7. N	7. C
8. B	8. covers	8. A	8. N	8. E
9. F	9. looked	9. A	9. V	9. D
10. D	10. turn	10. D	10. V	10. B

Comprehensive Test #5 Answer Key

Section I	Section II	Section III	Section IV	Section V
1. E	1. mark	1. A	1. N	1. F
2. J	2. minded	2. B	2. V	2. H
3. I	3. parking	3. A	3. V	3. J
4. H	4. rolling	4. D	4. N	4. B
5. F	5. shock	5. C	5. N	5. A
6. D	6. sign	6. B	6. V	6. I
7. C	7. point	7. A	7. V	7. E
8. A	8. reported	8. C	8. N	8. C
9. B	9. pick	9. C	9. N	9. D
10. G	10. plant	10. B	10. V	10. G

Master Verb List

PURE REGULAR VERBS

The following list of Pure Regular Verbs can be conjugated in the same manner. Try to learn their different meanings and various uses. Not all the verbs have been conjugated in this book. Only verbs in bold type have been conjugated.

A

absorb	absorbs	absorbing	absorbed	absorbed
accept	accepts	accepting	accepted	accepted
act	acts	acting	acted	acted
add	adds	adding	added	added
adjust	adjusts	adjusting	adjusted	adjusted
adopt	adopts	adopting	adopted	adopted
affect	affects	affecting	affected	affected
afford	affords	affording	afforded	afforded
aim	aims	aiming	aimed	aimed
allow	allows	allowing	allowed	allowed
answer	answers	answering	answered	answered
appear	appears	appearing	appeared	appeared
applaud	applauds	applauding	applauded	applauded
arm	arms	arming	armed	armed
ask	asks	asking	asked	asked
attack	attacks	attacking	attacked	attacked
attempt	attempts	attempting	attempted	attempted
attend	attends	attending	attended	attended
attract	attracts	attracting	attracted	attracted
avoid	avoids	avoiding	avoided	avoided

B

back	backs	backing	backed	backed
bang	bangs	banging	banged	banged
bank	banks	banking	banked	banked
bark	barks	barking	barked	barked
belong	belongs	belonging	belonged	belonged
benefit	benefits	benefiting	benefited	benefited
bill	bills	billing	billed	billed
blink	blinks	blinking	blinked	blinked
block	blocks	blocking	blocked	blocked
bluff	bluffs	bluffing	bluffed	bluffed
board	boards	boarding	boarded	boarded
boil	boils	boiling	boiled	boiled
bomb	bombs	bombing	bombed	bombed
borrow	borrows	borrowing	borrowed	borrowed
bother	bothers	bothering	bothered	bothered
bow	bows	bowing	bowed	bowed
bowl	bowls	bowling	bowled	bowled
broil	broils	broiling	broiled	broiled
bump	bumps	bumping	bumped	bumped
button	buttons	buttoning	buttoned	buttoned
burp	burps	burping	burped	burped

C

call	calls	calling	called	called
calm	calms	calming	calmed	calmed
camp	camps	camping	camped	camped
cheat	cheats	cheating	cheated	cheated
check	checks	checking	checked	checked
cheer	cheers	cheering	cheered	cheered
chew	chews	chewing	chewed	chewed
chill	chills	chilling	chilled	chilled
claim	claims	claiming	claimed	claimed
clean	cleans	cleaning	cleaned	cleaned

clear	clears	clearing	cleared	cleared
climb	climbs	climbing	climbed	climbed
collect	collects	collecting	collected	collected
comb	combs	combing	combed	combed
command	commands	commanding	commanded	commanded
complain	complains	complaining	complained	complained
conceal	conceals	concealing	concealed	concealed
confirm	confirms	confirming	confirmed	confirmed
connect	connects	connecting	connected	connected
consent	consents	consenting	consented	consented
consider	considers	considering	considered	considered
contain	contains	containing	contained	contained
cook	cooks	cooking	cooked	cooked
cool	cools	cooling	cooled	cooled
correct	corrects	correcting	corrected	corrected
cough	coughs	coughing	coughed	coughed
count	counts	counting	counted	counted
cover	covers	covering	covered	covered
crack	cracks	cracking	cracked	cracked
crawl	crawls	crawling	crawled	crawled
curl	curls	curling	curled	curled

D

defeat	defeats	defeating	defeated	defeated
defend	defends	defending	defended	defended
delay	delays	delaying	delayed	delayed
deliver	delivers	delivering	delivered	delivered
demand	demands	demanding	demanded	demanded
depart	departs	departing	departed	departed
depend	depends	depending	depended	depended
deposit	deposits	depositing	deposited	deposited
destroy	destroys	destroying	destroyed	destroyed
develop	develops	developing	developed	developed
dial	dials	dialing	dialed	dialed

diet	diets	dieting	dieted	dieted
direct	directs	directing	directed	directed
disappear	disappears	disappearing	disappeared	disappeared
disappoint	disappoints	disappointing	disappointed	disappointed
disconnect	disconnects	disconnecting	disconnected	disconnected
discover	discovers	discovering	discovered	discovered
disgust	disgusts	disgusting	disgusted	disgusted
disturb	disturbs	disturbing	disturbed	disturbed
doubt	doubts	doubting	doubted	doubted
drill	drills	drilling	drilled	drilled
drown	drowns	drowning	drowned	drowned
duck	ducks	ducking	ducked	ducked
dust	dusts	dusting	dusted	dusted

E

earn	earns	earning	earned	earned
elect	elects	electing	elected	elected
end	ends	ending	ended	ended
enjoy	enjoys	enjoying	enjoyed	enjoyed
enter	enters	entering	entered	entered
equal	equals	equaling	equaled	equaled
exhaust	exhausts	exhausting	exhausted	exhausted
exit	exits	exiting	exited	exited
expand	expands	expanding	expanded	expanded
expect	expects	expecting	expected	expected
experiment	experiments	experimenting	experimented	experimented
explain	explains	explaining	explained	explained
explode	explodes	exploding	exploded	exploded
export	exports	exporting	exported	exported

F

fail	fails	failing	failed	failed
fasten	fastens	fastening	fastened	fastened
fill	fills	filling	filled	filled

float	floats	floating	floated	floated
flood	floods	flooding	flooded	flooded
fold	folds	folding	folded	folded
follow	follows	following	followed	followed
fool	fools	fooling	fooled	fooled
form	forms	forming	formed	formed
forward	forwards	forwarding	forwarded	forwarded
frown	frowns	frowning	frowned	frowned

G

gain	gains	gaining	gained	gained
gather	gathers	gathering	gathered	gathered
golf	golfs	golfing	golfed	golfed
gossip	gossips	gossiping	gossiped	gossiped
greet	greets	greeting	greeted	greeted
grill	grills	grilling	grilled	grilled

H

hack	hacks	hacking	hacked	hacked
hail	hails	hailing	hailed	hailed
hammer	hammers	hammering	hammered	hammered
hand	hands	handing	handed	handed
hang	*meaning:* to be suspended by the neck			
	hangs	hanging	hanged	hanged
happen	happens	happening	happened	happened
haul	hauls	hauling	hauled	hauled
head	heads	heading	headed	headed
heal	heals	healing	healed	healed
heat	heats	heating	heated	heated
help	helps	helping	helped	helped
hiccup	hiccups	hiccuping	hiccuped	hiccuped
hint	hints	hinting	hinted	hinted
hook	hooks	hooking	hooked	hooked
hunt	hunts	hunting	hunted	hunted

I

import	imports	importing	imported	imported
inform	informs	informing	informed	informed
insist	insists	insisting	insisted	insisted
instruct	instructs	instructing	instructed	instructed
intend	intends	intending	intended	intended
interview	interviews	interviewing	interviewed	interviewed
introduce	introduces	introducing	introduced	introduced
iron	irons	ironing	ironed	ironed

J

jerk	jerks	jerking	jerked	jerked
join	joins	joining	joined	joined
jump	jumps	jumping	jumped	jumped

K

kick	kicks	kicking	kicked	kicked
kill	kills	killing	killed	killed
knock	knocks	knocking	knocked	knocked

L

land	lands	landing	landed	landed
last	lasts	lasting	lasted	lasted
laugh	laughs	laughing	laughed	laughed
leak	leaks	leaking	leaked	leaked
leap	leaps	leaping	leaped	leaped
learn	learns	learning	learned	learned
lick	licks	licking	licked	licked
lift	lifts	lifting	lifted	lifted
listen	listens	listening	listened	listened
litter	litters	littering	littered	littered
load	loads	loading	loaded	loaded
lock	locks	locking	locked	locked
look	looks	looking	looked	looked

M

mail	mails	mailing	mailed	mailed
major	majors	majoring	majored	majored
mark	marks	marking	marked	marked
market	markets	marketing	marketed	marketed
matter	matters	mattering	mattered	mattered
melt	melts	melting	melted	melted
mention	mentions	mentioning	mentioned	mentioned
mind	minds	minding	minded	minded
mount	mounts	mounting	mounted	mounted

N

nail	nails	nailing	nailed	nailed
need	needs	needing	needed	needed
neglect	neglects	neglecting	neglected	neglected

O

object	objects	objecting	objected	objected
offer	offers	offering	offered	offered
oil	oils	oiling	oiled	oiled
open	opens	opening	opened	opened
order	orders	ordering	ordered	ordered
own	owns	owning	owned	owned

P

pack	packs	packing	packed	packed
park	parks	parking	parked	parked
paint	paints	painting	painted	painted
part	parts	parting	parted	parted
peek	peeks	peeking	peeked	peeked
peel	peels	peeling	peeled	peeled
pick	picks	picking	picked	picked
plant	plants	planting	planted	planted
play	plays	playing	played	played

point	points	pointing	pointed	pointed
pound	pounds	pounding	pounded	pounded
pour	pours	pouring	poured	poured
pray	prays	praying	prayed	prayed
present	presents	presenting	presented	presented
pretend	pretends	pretending	pretended	pretended
prevent	prevents	preventing	prevented	prevented
print	prints	printing	printed	printed
profit	profits	profiting	profited	profited
protest	protests	protesting	protested	protested
puff	puffs	puffing	puffed	puffed
pull	pulls	pulling	pulled	pulled
pump	pumps	pumping	pumped	pumped

Q

question	questions	questioning	questioned	questioned

R

raid	raids	raiding	raided	raided
rain	rains	raining	rained	rained
recall	recalls	recalling	recalled	recalled
recommend	recommends	recommending	recommended	recommended
record	records	recording	recorded	recorded
reject	rejects	rejecting	rejected	rejected
remain	remains	remaining	remained	remained
remark	remarks	remarking	remarked	remarked
remember	remembers	remembering	remembered	remembered
remind	reminds	reminding	reminded	reminded
rent	rents	renting	rented	rented
repair	repairs	repairing	repaired	repaired
repeat	repeats	repeating	repeated	repeated
report	reports	reporting	reported	reported
request	requests	requesting	requested	requested
resent	resents	resenting	resented	resented

resist	resists	resisting	resisted	resisted
respond	responds	responding	responded	responded
rest	rests	resting	rested	rested
retreat	retreats	retreating	retreated	retreated
return	returns	returning	returned	returned
review	reviews	reviewing	reviewed	reviewed
riot	riots	rioting	rioted	rioted
risk	risks	risking	risked	risked
roast	roasts	roasting	roasted	roasted
rock	rocks	rocking	rocked	rocked
roll	rolls	rolling	rolled	rolled
row	rows	rowing	rowed	rowed
ruin	ruins	ruining	ruined	ruined

S

sail	sails	sailing	sailed	sailed
sand	sands	sanding	sanded	sanded
scold	scolds	scolding	scolded	scolded
scream	screams	screaming	screamed	screamed
screw	screws	screwing	screwed	screwed
season	seasons	seasoning	seasoned	seasoned
seem	seems	seeming	seemed	seemed
shampoo	shampoos	shampooing	shampooed	shampooed
shock	shocks	shocking	shocked	shocked
shout	shouts	shouting	shouted	shouted
shovel	shovels	shoveling	shoveled	shoveled
shower	showers	showering	showered	showered
sign	signs	signing	signed	signed
simmer	simmers	simmering	simmered	simmered
ski	skis	skiing	skied	skied
slow	slows	slowing	slowed	slowed
smell	smells	smelling	smelled	smelled
sneak	sneaks	sneaking	sneaked	sneaked
snow	snows	snowing	snowed	snowed

soak	soaks	soaking	soaked	soaked
sound	sounds	sounding	sounded	sounded
spank	spanks	spanking	spanked	spanked
spell	spells	spelling	spelled	spelled
spill	spills	spilling	spilled	spilled
spoil	spoils	spoiling	spoiled	spoiled
spray	sprays	spraying	sprayed	sprayed
squirt	squirts	squirting	squirted	squirted
stain	stains	staining	stained	stained
start	starts	starting	started	started
stay	stays	staying	stayed	stayed
steam	steams	steaming	steamed	steamed
subtract	subtracts	subtracting	subtracted	subtracted
succeed	succeeds	succeeding	succeeded	succeeded
suck	sucks	sucking	sucked	sucked
suggest	suggests	suggesting	suggested	suggested
suit	suits	suiting	suited	suited
surf	surfs	surfing	surfed	surfed
swallow	swallows	swallowing	swallowed	swallowed

T

talk	talks	talking	talked	talked
tend	tends	tending	tended	tended
test	tests	testing	tested	tested
thank	thanks	thanking	thanked	thanked
threaten	threatens	threatening	threatened	threatened
tighten	tightens	tightening	tightened	tightened
toast	toasts	toasting	toasted	toasted
tour	tours	touring	toured	toured
tow	tows	towing	towed	towed
track	tracks	tracking	tracked	tracked
train	trains	training	trained	trained
travel	travels	traveling	traveled	traveled
treat	treats	treating	treated	treated

trick	tricks	tricking	tricked	tricked
trust	trusts	trusting	trusted	trusted
turn	turns	turning	turned	turned
twist	twists	twisting	twisted	twisted

U

| uncover | uncovers | uncovering | uncovered | uncovered |
| unfasten | unfastens | unfastening | unfastened | unfastened |

V

vacuum	vacuums	vacuuming	vacuumed	vacuumed
visit	visits	visiting	visited	visited
volunteer	volunteers	volunteering	volunteered	volunteered
vomit	vomits	vomiting	vomited	vomited

W

wait	waits	waiting	waited	waited
walk	walks	walking	walked	walked
want	wants	wanting	wanted	wanted
warm	warms	warming	warmed	warmed
warn	warns	warning	warned	warned
water	waters	watering	watered	watered
weigh	weighs	weighing	weighed	weighed
whisper	whispers	whispering	whispered	whispered
wink	winks	winking	winked	winked
wonder	wonders	wondering	wondered	wondered
work	works	working	worked	worked
wreck	wrecks	wrecking	wrecked	wrecked

Y

yank	yanks	yanking	yanked	yanked
yawn	yawns	yawning	yawned	yawned
yell	yells	yelling	yelled	yelled